ART

CurriculumBank

KEY STAGE ONE
SCOTTISH LEVELS A-B

ART

STEPHEN BUGG

POSTER PACK

A poster pack to accompany this book is available from Scholastic. Comprising four full colour A2 posters, the pack provides a useful resource to enable teachers to fully exploit activities described in this book.

The four posters are:
Mother and Child by Mary Cassatt;
The Vicar and his Sister by Peter Rush;
Irises by Vincent Van Gogh;
My Body by Henry Moore and Alberto Giacometti.

These have all been previously published in *Art & Craft*, Scholastic.

The Curriculum Bank Art KS1 poster pack can be purchased separately from: Scholastic Educational Books, Westfield Road, Southam, Warwickshire CV33 0JH, Please quote ISBN 0 590 53753 9.

Introduction

Scholastic Curriculum Bank is a series for all primary teachers, providing an essential planning tool for devising comprehensive schemes of work as well as an easily accessible and varied bank of practical, classroom-tested activities with photocopiable resources.

Designed to help planning for and implementation of progression, differentiation and assessment, *Scholastic Curriculum Bank* offers a structured range of stimulating activities with clearly stated learning objectives that reflect the programmes of study, and detailed lesson plans that allow busy teachers to put ideas into practice with the minimum amount of preparation time. The photocopiable sheets that accompany many of the activities provide ways of integrating purposeful application of knowledge and skills, differentiation, assessment and record-keeping.

Opportunities for formative assessment are highlighted within the activities where appropriate, while separate summative assessment activities give guidelines for analysis and subsequent action. Ways of using information technology for different purposes and in different contexts, as a tool for communicating and handling information and as a means of investigating, are integrated into the activities where appropriate, and more explicit guidance is provided at the end of the book.

The series covers all the primary curriculum subjects, with separate books for Key Stages 1 and 2 or Scottish Levels A–B and C–E. It can be used as a flexible resource with any scheme, to fulfil National Curriculum and Scottish 5–14 requirements and to provide children with a variety of different learning experiences that will lead to effective acquisition of skills and knowledge.

SCHOLASTIC CURRICULUM BANK ART

The *Scholastic Curriculum Bank Art* books help teachers to plan comprehensive and structured coverage of the art curriculum, and help children to develop the required skills and understanding through practical activities.

Each book covers one key stage. There is one book for Key Stage 1/Scottish Levels A–B and one book for Key Stage 2/Scottish Levels C–E. These books reflect the programmes of study for Art in the National Curriculum for England and Wales, and in the Scottish National Guidelines.

Art is interpreted to cover art, craft and design and the ideas in this book aim to provide a comprehensive coverage of opportunities for individual and group working arrangements, a range of skills and techniques and an appreciation of work in a wide variety of genres and styles.

Lesson plans

Detailed lesson plans, under clear headings, are given for each activity. They provide ideas for a wide variety of activities covering art, craft and design. The structure for each lesson plan is as follows:

Activity title box

The information in the title box at the beginning of each activity outlines the following key aspects:

▲ *Activity title and learning objective* – Each activity has one or more clearly stated learning objectives, given in bold italics. These learning objectives break down aspects of the programmes of study into manageable teaching and learning units, and their purpose is to aid planning for breadth and balance. They can easily be referenced to the National Curriculum and Scottish 5–14 requirements by using the overview grids at the end of this section (pages 11 to 14).

▲ *Class organisation/likely duration* – Icons 👫 and 🕐

signpost the suggested group size and the approximate amount of time required to complete it. Timing arrangements are by their nature arbitrary, as many factors are involved (including the children's previous skills and knowledge). In addition many activities have untimed follow-up sessions.

Previous skills/knowledge needed

Information is given here when it is necessary for the children to have developed particular skills, experienced certain activities or acquired special knowledge before the activity.

Key background information

The information here is intended to set the scene and provide helpful guidance for the teacher. The guidance may relate to children's learning, to teachers' knowledge of art or to both.

Preparation

Advice is given where it is necessary either to prepare the children for the activity or to collect and prepare materials before working with the children. It is often useful to have tried out some of the activities prior to the session. This ensures that the teacher has a knowledge of the types of activities the children will wish to try out and raises awareness of the difficulties they may encounter.

Resources needed

All the equipment, materials and photocopiable sheets needed to carry out the activity are listed here, so that the children or the teacher can gather them together easily before the beginning of the teaching session.

What to do
Easy-to-follow, step-by-step instructions are given for the activity, including (where appropriate) suggested points for discussion with the children. Several activities are broken down into a series of stages or sessions to achieve the overall aim. Others have further sessions to develop the work.

Suggestion(s) for extension/support
Where possible, ways of providing for easy differentiation are suggested. Ways of offering support to less able pupils and ideas to extend the more able are provided.

Assessment opportunities
Each lesson plan has clearly stated assessment opportunities which relate directly to the learning objectives for that activity and provide the framework for ongoing assessment. By taking advantage of these assessment opportunities, teachers can be reassured that the stated learning objectives have been covered.

Opportunities for IT
Where opportunities for IT applications arise, these are briefly outlined. Pages 158 to 159 provide general advice on IT and art, with reference to suitable types of program. The chart on page 159 lists specific areas of IT covered in the activities.

Looking at works of art
Suggestions are given for existing works of art which will enhance the children's understanding of a theme. Note that where the text recommends 'Looking at the work of other artists' this can equally refer to art students' work as to the paintings of famous artists such as Van Gogh or Picasso.

Where you will find works of art and useful resources:
▲ poster packs produced to accompany these *Curriculum Bank Art* books;
▲ published art books or posters available from other sources, including *Art & Craft magazine* (Scholastic);
▲ twentieth-century art books (which would be invaluable);
▲ print packs of famous art works – available at quite low cost on topics such as portraits, landscapes, buildings, animals and so on.

Display ideas
Suggestions for displaying the children's completed work are provided in this section.

Reference to photocopiable sheet(s)
Where activities include photocopiable activity sheets, these are referred to here and a miniature version is shown.

Photocopiable activity sheets
Many of the activities include photocopiable ideas which provide extensions or suggest alternative ways of working. With some, the children are required to develop imaginatively the briefest of beginnings to a drawing and in others to use the information provided as a stimulus for the development of a short project. In a few, however, they are asked to add colour or texture to the actual photocopiable. While this can be an appropriate activity, the learning objective needs to be very clear. 'Colouring in' as an end in itself is unlikely to be a valuable activity and should seldom be asked of the children.

Some sheets may be used for assessment purposes and would be useful as records to include in portfolios of children's work to monitor their progression in art.

Cross-curricular links
Cross-curricular links are identified on a simple grid (see page 160) which cross-references particular areas of study in art to the work which could be undertaken in other subject areas.

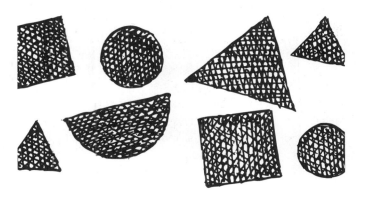

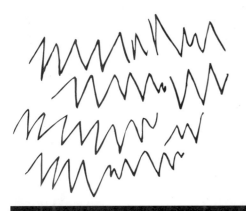  

ART AND THE NATIONAL CURRICULUM

The National Curriculum identifies Attainment Targets and Programmes of Study for art which clearly re-emphasises the point that, along with all other subjects, art needs to be taught through a structured scheme of work. The teaching which you provide needs to be well organised to ensure continuity and progression and to take into account the individual needs of the children. Without carefully planned opportunities and sensitive teaching, the progress made by the children will be limited.

When planning an art curriculum for Key Stage 1 it is necessary to ensure the children will be:

▲ given opportunities to express feelings and ideas, record observations and make images and artefacts;

▲ given access to a wide range of experiences and materials;

▲ taught to use the visual elements;

▲ able to develop their visual literacy;

▲ introduced to the work of artists, designers and crafts people.

By fulfilling these requirements you can ensure that all children have the opportunity to develop to their full potential.

Investigating and making

Art is an essentially practical activity through which children come to understand more about the world in which they live. They need to question what they see and to investigate further in order to increase this understanding. It is important therefore, to provide the time, opportunities and incentives to 'look'. From looking, whether at flowers, people, buildings or the work of other artists, comes understanding. Looking, touching, questioning, collecting, organising and selecting are all important art activities.

The ability to record these observations further develops the children's understanding. Drawing from direct observation is therefore at the heart of artistic activity. Children require regular opportunities to sketch, make notes and draw in order to help them make sense of their observations and to develop their confidence to express themselves clearly.

Drawing to record observations is not, however, the only activity children need to undertake for they must also be given opportunities to express moods and feelings. The visual image can speak more loudly than words, not only for young children who have not reached the age when they can express themselves fluently through writing, but for adults also. The need to express anger, outrage, fear and grief, happiness and joy, are important elements in all the arts. Indeed, some of the most poignant statements on human suffering come from the drawings of children and the paintings of great artists.

There are times also when children require opportunities to design and make artefacts, whether this be a pattern for a book jacket, a junk model or a salt dough relief. The National Curriculum identifies only art in the title but then immediately makes it clear that art must encompass art, craft and design.

The activities described in this book ensure that the children will undertake a wide range of art, craft and design work. They will ensure that they regularly draw and sketch, use colour and in particular paint, work with dough, clay and construction materials, use a range of collage materials, and collect, select and organise materials and information. They will be required to regularly work from observation but they will also be given the opportunity to express feelings and experiences and to produce patterns, shapes and forms. They will be constantly required to find their own solutions and to draw and represent their own interpretations of the world as they see, feel and experience it. It is developing

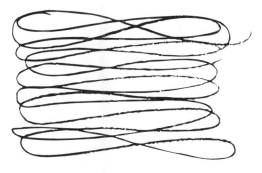
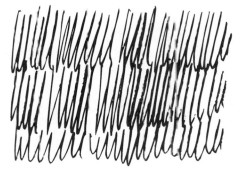
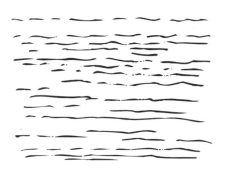

their confidence to record and express the world in which they live that is at the heart of these activities.

Developing skills

When children undertake these practical activities the learning objective needs to be clear and they need to understand the purpose of the activity. In order for the children to develop confidence and not be frustrated when producing their art work, they need to be taught a wide range of skills, in particular how to use the visual and tactile elements. In other words they need regular opportunities to learn about, and how to use: pattern, texture, colour, line, tone, shape, form and space, in order to be better able to express, record and make images and artefacts.

Through their manipulation of these elements the children will develop their visual perception and language. They will learn, for example, not only to use different types of line in their own art work but also to talk about linear qualities in the work of others.

As with teaching reading or number, it is important that there is a consistent approach to the teaching of art. If, for example, colour mixing is introduced in the reception class, and the children become used to working with a specified range of colours, then the same approach needs to be followed at Key Stage 1 so that the children can, with confidence, further develop these skills. Each of the visual elements needs to be returned to at regular intervals and teachers need to refer to them in their discussions with the class or group, both when introducing an activity and when evaluating outcomes.

The children also need to be introduced to a range of craft and technical skills, for example, the ability to make a coiled pot or to make a textile hanging, or the ability to mix paint or to glue objects together.

In order to teach children this wide range of skills a variety of teaching strategies are required. The children will need to be taught through sensitive questioning, demonstrations, technical support, receiving information, being introduced to a variety of differing stimuli and through the evaluation of their finished work.

Understanding and knowledge

It is also important to give children the opportunity to explore the work of other artists. Through their observations and discussions they will come to understand and appreciate not only the work of artists, crafts people and designers, but their own work as well.

Looking at works of art needs to be a voyage of discovery. It requires intense observation, and should be supplemented by the asking of questions, the offering of theories, the sharing of thoughts and by responding to the views and thoughts of others.

Using the poster pack accompanying this book, and taking the Mary Cassatt poster *Mother and Child* as an example, the children (from looking at this work) will develop their understanding not only of how one artist explains the relationship between a mother and her baby, but how one particular artist uses colour, line, shape and pattern in the execution of the work. From these observations the children will comprehend their own drawings in a different light.

As the children build their understanding of art and the processes and language of art so too will they develop and build their knowledge.

TEACHING ART

Starting school

Before they start compulsory school all children will have been exposed to art in the widest sense. They will certainly have started to make marks on paper with pencils or crayons, may have made some models using recycled materials and will probably have moulded play dough or Plasticine into interesting shapes.

On starting school, children should have explored colour, texture, shape, form and space in 2D and 3D, as recommended under the School Curriculum and Assessment Authority's Desirable Outcomes for Creative Development. They should also have had experience of a range of materials, tools and instruments to express their ideas and feelings.

So, on entering school most children will be equipped to develop and extend these early skills. The teacher's job is to stimulate their imagination and harness their enthusiasm to produce an exciting and colourful range of art work.

Learning and teaching

Between the ages of five and seven the vast majority of children make great strides with their drawing and painting. This development often appears almost intuitive, for when we observe the art work of a wide range of young children the many similarities and characteristics in their drawings and paintings quickly become apparent.

It is possible to state this development quite simply: when they enter school most young children can draw people symbolically, to what appears a prescribed format, with circular head, rectangular body, arms outstretched and long spindly legs. By the end of the key stage their drawing of people will have progressed to the point where some children will be producing recognisable portraits of friends, showing their ability to record analytically.

Similarly they begin this period using paint arbitrarily and will develop to produce paintings demonstrating their growing ability to mix a wide range of colours.

There are, however, dangers in seeing the development of children's drawing in such simplistic terms. Whilst there are clear and very similar stages through which each child will pass, this progress is at a widely varying pace. There will be an equal spread of variance directly comparable to that which we observe in young children's reading ability. Some children will therefore enter school with emerging evidence of their ability to record analytically, whilst some will not pass beyond the earliest signs of symbolic drawing. Planning to meet the needs of this wide range of ability is therefore one of the biggest challenges which confronts the KS1 teacher.

This developmental sequence can lead to the conclusion that young children need only the opportunity to engage in a variety of art work for them to develop their artistic ability, albeit at different speeds. Where this thinking is prevalent, art lessons are often characterised by groups of children undertaking 'self maintaining' exercises with little formal input.

Whilst there may be some occasions where this is appropriate, in many art sessions children will need to be taught directly. They need to be taught how to look, investigate, record, use technical processes, evaluate, select and design. They need to be constantly challenged and stimulated, to become confident in their handling and use of materials, and to develop a precise language which they can use to explain and talk about art work (their own and others'). In meeting these needs lies a major problem for the teacher in how best to organise these learning experiences so that children have access to the direct teaching they require.

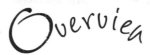

Learning objective	PoS/AO	Content	Type of activity	Page
Line				
To learn about a variety of ways of making lines and marks, using various media.	8e, f. *Using media Level A*	Experimenting with drawing a wide variety of lines.	Whole class in small groups with an adult.	16
To develop different ways of making lines, in particular to create movement.	8e, f. *Using visual elements Level A*	Exploring how to make lines give the feeling of movement.	Whole class.	18
To develop the ability to express and communicate moods and feelings through drawing.	8a, e, f; 9d. *Communicating Level B*	Exploring how lines can express a mood or feeling.	Whole class; working individually.	21
To develop the ability to observe, and to record observations accurately.	8a, b, e, f. *Investigating visually and recording Level B*	Investigating and drawing vegetables and fruit looking for interesting lines and shapes.	Whole class or group work.	24
To introduce ways of using line to explain how things work. To be analytical when observing and to record findings using diagrams and drawings.	8a, b, c. *As above*	Observational drawings showing how various parts of a bike work.	Small groups or whole class.	26
To become more aware of the immediate environment, using observations to extend drawing ability.	8a, c, d, d, f. *As above*	Looking at how lines make shapes and at shapes found in the classroom.	Small groups; whole class with other adult help.	29
To develop the use of line through exploring the work of one artist. To understand how artists use line in their paintings.	8a, e, f; 9b, c, d, e. *Observing, reflecting, describing and responding*	From studying Mary Cassatt, to make observed drawings of figures concentrating on the quality of line.	Whole class or small groups.	31
To develop the ability to use differing qualities of line to express thoughts, feelings and moods.	7e; 8a, d, e, f. *Creating and designing Level B*	Imaginary drawing on the theme of Under the sea. Emphasis on line and shape.	Small groups or whole class.	34
Colour				
To be able to use primary colours to mix a wide range of other colours. To understand the basic processes for mixing colours.	8d, e. *Using visual elements Level A*	Learning to mix colours working from the primaries.	Individual, pairs or small groups.	38
To collect, match and identify colours, and to use the outcome to produce colour patterns.	8b, c, e. *As above*	Collecting examples of colour. Mixing paints in chosen colour.	Whole class or small groups.	40
To accurately record colours from direct observation and to develop colour mixing skills.	7e; 8a, d, e. *As above Level B*	Colour mixing, painting enlarged sections of flower or fruit.	Small groups (four to eight children).	42

Learning objective	PoS/AO	Content	Type of activity	Page
To develop the use of colour to express moods and feelings.	7e; 8a, d, e, f. *Creating and designing Level B*	Using colour to express mood through imaginative paintings of skies and seas.	Small group or whole class.	44
To increase the range of ways in which colour can be used.	8a, c, d, e, f. *Using media Level B*	Colour sketchbooks; applying colour to paper in various ways.	Whole class or small group.	47
To develop the knowledge and understanding of how a famous artist uses colour and to use this understanding to improve our own painting.	7e, f; 8a, d, e. *Observing, reflecting, describing and responding Level B*	Discussing a Van Gogh painting and then applying colour in a similar manner.	Whole class.	49
To understand the importance and value of drawing from direct observation. To use colour creatively in a controlled manner.	8a, b, c, e. *Investigating visually and responding Level B*	Observing and drawing doors. Painting using complementaries and tones of one colour.	Whole class or small group.	52
To develop the ability to use colour in design.	7e, f; 8c, d, e f. *Create and design Level B*	To design and paint shapes to decorate a box on the theme of the sea.	Small group or whole class.	54
Pattern				
To select and organise shapes to make patterns through simple printing processes.	8d, e, f. *Using media Level A*	Simple printmaking making patterns using hands and small objects.	Small group.	58
To develop the ability to identify simple patterns.	8d, e, f. *As above.*	Developing printing skills working from simple shapes.	Whole class; small groups for printing work.	60
To develop the ability to see pattern in everyday life. To develop the ability to select, arrange and organise pattern.	8a, c, e, f. *As above Level B*	Looking for pattern in houses and buildings. Designing a pattern of houses on an estate.	Whole class; working individually and in groups.	62
To create pattern through imaginative drawing. To develop collaborative working.	8a, d, e. *Creating and designing Level B*	Pattern in imaginative landscapes. Using shapes to create interesting patterns.	Whole class.	65
To identify the wide range of patterns that can be achieved from experimenting with simple mathematical shapes.	7e, f; 8c, e, f. *Observing, reflecting, describing and responding Level B*	Look at the work of Klimt and use similar style to create vibrant patterns.	Whole class or small group.	67

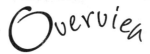

Learning objective	PoS/AO	Content	Type of activity	Page
To understand the reoccurrence of pattern in nature. To develop the ability to observe and record directly from nature.	8a, c, e. *Investigating visually and recording Level B*	Detailed observation of plants prior to repeating drawing of plant shapes to make patterns.	Whole class or small groups.	70
To identify the wide range of patterns to be found in people and in the clothes they wear.	7e; 8a, c, e. *As above*	Drawing from observation and painting.	Whole class or small groups.	72
To identify the shapes and patterns associated with letter formation, and to explore the potential for art work.	8b, d, e. *Using visual elements Level B*	Looking at patterns in letters and numbers through overlaying and working with mirror images.	Whole class.	75
Texture				
To understand the importance of texture in producing art work.	8a, d, e. *Using visual elements Level B*	Feeling unknown objects and describing the texture through drawing.	Whole class or small groups.	78
To identify some of the wide range of textures in the natural and man-made world, and to be able to develop art work from these observations.	8a, b, c, d, e. *As above*	Exploring textures in natural and man-made environment through a series of rubbings and of making simple casts.	Small group or whole class.	80
To identify the wide range of textures in the bark from trees. To develop an understanding of simple processes involved in working with clay.	8d, e. *As above*	Exploring texture through making simple clay relief tiles.	Small group.	82
To develop the ability to represent texture using a range of media and working from direct observations.	7f; 8a, c, d, e. *Investigating visually and recording Level B*	Looking at the surface of fruit, vegetables or animals. Recording using a variety of media and processes.	Whole class for first task; small group for second, if space is limited.	84
To explore the importance of texture and pattern in the art process.	8b, d, e. *As above*	Making a collage and printing to reveal texture.	Whole class or small group. Small group for printing.	85
To explore the basic qualities of weaving using a variety of materials.	8c, d, e. *Using media Level B*	Weaving using materials, wools and found objects.	Small group or whole class.	87
To explore the uses of a wide variety of textures to create a relief portrait. To raise awareness of the physical properties of ageing.	7e, f; 8d, e, f. *Creating and designing Level B*	Clay and papier mâché work based on the Peter Rush poster 'The Vicar and his Sister'.	Whole class or small group.	89
To use a wide range of textures to enhance pattern work.	8b, c, d, e. *Using visual elements Level B*	Building up textures based on study of patterned cloth.	Small group or whole class.	91

Learning objective	PoS/AO	Content	Type of activity	Page
Form				
To explore the relationship between shape and form using simple paper cut outs.	8c, d, e, f. *As above*	Making paper boxes decorated with folded, curled and torn papers.	Small groups.	94
To develop motor skills required to manipulate malleable materials. To be able to express personal views using a 3D material.	8d, e. *Using media Level B*	Using salt dough to make relief designs of houses.	Small groups.	96
To further develop manipulative skills and to understand some of the basic properties of clay.	8d, e, f. *As above*	Moulding clay and making simple pinch pots.	Small groups.	97
To develop understanding of three-dimensional pattern through using and organising three-dimensional objects.	8c, d, e. *As above*	Using found objects and construction materials to make sculpture.	Small groups.	99
To record observations accurately and quickly. To develop collaborative ways of working and sharing ideas. To develop pattern making and three-dimensional skills.	7e, f; 8a, d, e, f. *Investigating visually and recording Level B*	Drawing quick sketches of figures and using patterns and shapes of people to create a mobile.	Whole class.	101
To improvise with a range of materials to create masks. To use the masks to create role-play situations.	7e, f; 8c, d, e, f. *As above*	Making masks of various sorts having first studied masks from around the world.	Small groups working in pairs.	104
To identify the characteristics in the work of a famous artist and to use the understanding and knowledge of the artist's work to inform future art work.	7e, f; 8d, e, f. *Observing, reflecting, describing and responding Level A*	Introduction to armatures, used to make textured figures in the style of Giacometti poster.	Small groups.	106
To be able to use clay in a functional way to make a pot. To develop manipulative skills and to increase awareness of form and pattern.	8d, e. *Using media Level B*	Developing clay skills to make simple coiled pots.	Small groups.	108

Line

From the moment children use a pencil to make a mark on paper they begin to use lines to express themselves. Early line drawings are often bold scribbles but as children begin to make representations of people and objects their use of line goes through various phases, ranging from strong and confident to very tentative. Without direction, a child will increasingly use line to express outline. All lines will tend to become of a consistent strength and uniformity. The purpose of the activities in this chapter is to make children aware of the wide range of ways in which line drawing can be used to communicate information and feelings.

Pencils and pens are not the only methods by which children can create lines and they need opportunities to explore other media. The activities described require experimentation with string, cut and torn paper, pastels and paints, often as a development from an initial drawing activity using a pencil.

From such exercises the children will be better able to express themselves when drawing from observation. They will come to realise that accuracy in drawing may equally be about showing the difference in weight between two objects, for example, the petal of a flower and a thick heavy stem, as in achieving corresponding proportions. Similarly they will realise that the lines used to express a calm and tranquil sea may be very different to those used to explain waves breaking during a howling gale. Looking at how artists use line to express feelings and emotions will further consolidate their practical work.

EXPERIMENTING WITH LINE

To learn about a variety of ways of making lines and marks, using various media.

†† *Whole class in small groups with an adult.*

🕐 *45 minutes; follow-up sessions.*

Previous skills/knowledge needed

This is an introductory activity, the children require no specific previous experience. However, they will all have had some practice of drawing and writing with pencils and crayons, and will have some knowledge of using different media on paper.

Key background information

Developing children's ability to use a variety of lines and marks when undertaking drawing is an important early stage in teaching art. Without experimenting children will almost always draw using a continuous solid line. They therefore require opportunities to try out a wide range of line and mark making to extend the scope of their skills.

Preparation

Practise drawing different types of line yourself before the lesson so that you are clear about the possibilities. If you are undertaking this art activity with the class for the first time, then it is worth allowing yourself five to ten minutes' practice using the same materials and equipment as you will ask the children to use. This clarifies the objectives and helps identify any potential difficulties. Involve any other adults who will be supporting the children at this stage.

Resources needed

Two or three sheets of A4 white activity paper per child, 2B or sketching pencils, chalk, charcoal, scissors, medium-sized pointed paintbrushes and black paint (preferably 'ready mixed').

What to do

Begin by handing out the paper and pencils and asking the children to draw various types of line using pencils on the paper. On the first sheet of paper ask them to draw a thick zigzagging line, a thin frail line, a swirling line and a 'very complicated' twisting, turning line. When they have tried this, discuss the range of lines they have made identifying particularly interesting ones.

On the second sheet of paper ask them to produce patterns of lines, trying four or five times to repeat a line they have drawn, but each time making a small change. Challenge them to make their patterns of lines represent a mood. For example, ask them what sort of lines they would draw if they were cross? Can they draw a series of lines which show happiness?

Continue by asking the children to fold their next piece of paper into four and to experiment by making a distinct type of line in each of the four squares. So, for example, they may produce a swirling, flowing line in the first square, whilst the second consists of short sharp lines with sharp angles, and the third has a whole series of lines which are all of varying thicknesses and strengths, depending on how hard they press. Again, one square may consist of a pattern in which they experiment with drawing very similar lines but pressing with their pencil with differing strengths to produce a range of tones.

Further sessions

Now that the children have been introduced to a range of ways of making lines or marks using a pencil, continue in further sessions by asking them to develop their line making using other media. They should try, for example, using charcoal on grey paper, chalk on black paper or alternatively using paint and brushes. If they choose to paint, advise them on how to load the brush with paint and how to control the brush mark as they make the required line on their paper.

Experiment further by asking them to produce simple collages, by cutting strips, bands and wavy lines using

scissors, and gluing these lines onto a background paper, to produce lively rhythmical patterns. They may also try making lines of varying thicknesses using torn paper to produce patterns which can be stuck onto a background sheet.

Making a monoprint

Start by doing a quick, simple drawing, the subject matter is unimportant. Roll out a small amount of water-based printing ink onto a board or piece of perspex to cover at least the same area as your drawing. The key to success is to ensure that the ink is virtually dry. If it is thick and sticky you are unlikely to achieve a successful print. Use sticky tape to attach a thin piece of white paper to the back of your drawing and lay both pieces on to the ink bed with the drawing facing up. Trace over your drawing. When finished lift the paper off the ink and discover a textured monoprint on the backing paper. The result can be extremely pleasing and enhance the qualities of the original drawing.

Suggestion(s) for extension

More able children may be able to develop their skills further using print, although when undertaking craft skills for the first time young children will obviously need adult support and close oversight. Show them how to stick string onto card and use it for printing, or how to draw lines and marks onto 'press print' or smooth polystyrene using a sharp implement and then rolling on ink and printing. An alternative way of producing interesting line prints can be achieved by rolling the ink directly onto a flat surface, making sure it is almost dry before laying on a piece of paper and then drawing onto the surface pressing hard to produce a monoprint. When the paper is lifted a textured print should be revealed on the

reverse. This process can be enhanced by asking the children to stick patches of coloured tissue papers onto the surface of the piece of paper before laying it onto the almost dry ink and then drawing on the reverse side.

Suggestion(s) for support

Constantly encourage the children to think hard about their line and mark making during the initial activities, stressing the need to produce as wide a range of marks as possible. There should however be no need for you to demonstrate. Where possible engage the support of an adult or non-teaching support assistant to help the children but not to do it for them!

Assessment opportunities

After each two or three line drawings discuss results with the children inviting them to point out which are the most successful. Retain the children's drawings so that they can be referred to again when necessary (they may be used to form the beginnings of a sketch book). Assess the final pictures by discussing with the children the various qualities of line they have achieved, for example, the rhythmic qualities in their patterns or the variations in texture of the lines in their monoprints.

Opportunities for IT

Extend the activity using an art package. Show the children how to draw lines either using the freehand tool (which allows curved lines to be drawn) or the straight line tool. To explore the effect of different weights show the children how to change the tool from either a pencil to a paint brush and how to select the appropriate thickness of pencil or brush to get the desired effect. The children can then explore the activities they have carried out using pencils or other mark marking tools; print out the final results. Very young children could use a touchscreen for this work where their finger becomes the line-making tool.

This work provides an excellent opportunity for children to talk about the advantages and disadvantages of using a computer for art work.

Looking at works of art

Picasso's drawings provide a wonderful starting point for discussing the qualities of line to be found in the work of famous artists. Leonardo's botanical drawings, and Van Gogh and Cézanne are also interesting to look at with young children. Some Chinese and Japanese paintings, particularly of plants, also demonstrate wonderful linear qualities. Ask the children to focus on the artist's use of line by asking them questions for example; Has the artist varied the thickness of the lines? Is there a sense of movement and direction to the lines? Do the lines appear to speed up or slow down as they travel across the paper?

Display ideas

Display the children's 'four square' drawings in blocks to emphasise the patterns they make. To display the children's monoprints, rather than cutting down the children's work to remove untidy or unfinished edges, ask them to draw a rectangle on a new piece of paper, cut it out to form a window and 'scan' over their prints so that they can select for themselves the area to be mounted. They can then window mount their prints for display.

MAKING IT MOVE

To develop different ways of making lines, in particular to create movement.

†† *Whole class.*

⏰ *60 minutes; follow-up sessions.*

Previous skills/knowledge needed

This activity is designed for young children with very little previous experience of drawing. It can be returned to at different times, to reinforce the children's understanding of the different ways of making lines. It is (along with Experimenting with line, page 16 and Exploring moods, page 21 one of three activities designed to widen children's use of mark making when drawing.

Key background information

Without teaching, the vast majority of children will draw in outlines pressing with equal thicknesses at all times. They need to be encouraged and given opportunities to experiment so that they learn the value of using a very wide range of marks to create different kinds of lines. Indeed, we often ask children to draw 'concrete' objects, for example a person, flower or plant, but seldom give them opportunities to draw using their imagination to show movement, mood or feeling. This activity develops further the children's ability to draw using a wide range of lines to create a feeling of movement.

Preparation

If you are undertaking this art activity with the class for the first time, allow five to ten minutes to practise yourself beforehand, using the same materials and equipment as will be given to the children. This clarifies the objectives, helps identify any potential difficulties and demonstrates some of the possible outcomes. If any other adults will be helping in your session, involve them at this stage too. Familiarise the children with the story of Hansel and Gretel. Photocopy pages 112 and 113, one of each per child.

Resources needed

Cheap white paper (better quality will be required if the children are to use paint), sketching pencils, coloured crayons, Plasticine, florist wire, coloured wools, adhesive, scissors, and card. Photocopiable pages 112 and 113.

What to do

Ask the children to think about how animals move. Encourage them to describe to you how a rabbit, frog, bee or snake moves. Let the children try out these movements using their fingers on the table to help them explain the way in which the animal moves. Encourage precision with words as well as with movements. You may even like to use a PE session to explore various types of whole-body movement.

Give each child two or three sheets of white paper, a sketching pencil and some coloured crayons. Ask them to draw lines going across the first sheet of paper which describe the movements of these various animals. They should attempt, by the pressure exerted with the pencil, to indicate differing speeds. Discuss their results, by asking them to look at each others' drawings and to see if they can tell which animal's movements are being depicted.

On the second sheet of paper ask the children to recall the story of Hansel and Gretel. Ask them to close their eyes and imagine they are lost in the wood. Can they imagine how they would run about amongst the trees, looking for a path they recognise, stopping and starting, running and walking? Ask them to now start with their pencils in the middle of their paper and very slowly and carefully try to describe, with the line of their pencil, how they begin to try to find their way through the imaginary trees. Can they show the different speeds at which they travel and how they go back and forth, going over the same ground more than once, before they eventually find the witch's house?

Similar ideas to use as a stimulus may include showing

water going downstream encountering differing obstacles as it goes, or the wind whistling through trees. Throughout the session discuss with the children the outcomes they arrive at and ask them to identify which are the most successful and why.

Hand out the photocopiable pages, one of each for each child, and let them work on these to develop their line-drawing skills to create more movement.

Further sessions

The children will quickly come to see that, where their work requires many lines, their line drawings make interesting patterns. In future sessions encourage the children to paint or draw the most interesting of their drawings. If the drawings have been done on poor quality paper the children will first need to redraw them on cartridge paper. This will also allow them to make any alterations they consider necessary to improve their pattern.

Patterns can also be repeated using different media. You may ask the children to roll out a long strip of Plasticine in order to create their lines in relief or to use coloured wools and to glue lines of wool down onto stiff card. Show them how to produce a three dimensional form by using pipe cleaners or florist wire which the children bend to create lines in the air. Spiralling lines may also be cut out, attached to thread, and left to hang, creating mobiles from their lines.

Suggestion(s) for extension

Once the children have experimented with drawing lines that not only twist and turn but also vary in thickness and tone, some children can use their new-found skills in further picture making. Ask them to draw a picture of clothes on the washing line blowing in the wind or a bonfire with the flames flickering and the smoke billowing.

Suggestion(s) for support

Ensure that there is good pace to the lesson. Be strict about the time limits and encourage the children to complete each task within a specified time. You will need to praise constantly examples where the children are achieving a range of interesting lines so that they quickly come to see the objective of the lesson.

Assessment opportunities

During the initial activity assessment will be undertaken through discussion with the whole class. Ask for example: Why does this one look so interesting? What could we do to this drawing to make the sense of movement more clear?

At the end of the first session assess the results. Are the children producing interesting drawings which they would benefit from continuing to develop, through a further lesson? If so, then continue with lines in various media or drawings of bonfires and washing lines. Be prepared to evaluate activities in mid programme and make adjustments to meet the needs of the children.

Opportunities for IT

The children could create their movement pictures using an art package. As well as knowing how to draw lines of different thicknesses they will need to be able to practise drawing good curved lines using the freehand tool. To add colours they will need to be shown how to select colours from a palette of available colours. Older or more able children could be given access to a much larger palette or even mix their own. Very young children or those with less well-developed motor skills could use a touchscreen to create their movement pictures.

Looking at works of art

A valuable resource for all schools is two or three good reference books on art. Flicking through any reference book on twentieth-century art you will discover a good variety of pictures where the artist has used a wide range of lines. If there is time to visit a library then the drawings of Picasso provide a wealth of examples of how to use line expressively. The Futurist artists (such as Boccioni and Balla) painting in Italy in the early twentieth century were also interested in movement and many of their paintings have repetitive rhythmical lines. Remember it is not necessary to like the picture or to understand its meaning before introducing the children to it. Be prepared to ask such questions as: What sort of lines has the artist used? Are the lines solid or broken? Can you trace the length of one particular line? How would you describe the lines to someone who was blind?

Display ideas

Display their pictures alongside simple questions. Ask the children whether they can guess what the lines describe, or whether they can tell whether they are fast or slow lines.

Reference to photocopiable sheets

A number of artists, including Klee and Miró, use lines to create delightful, comic images. Working on this theme, ask the children to complete photocopiable page 112 using short, expressive lines to show birds in various stages of flight. The birds already drawn should encourage the children to experiment rather than attempt to draw realistic interpretations.

The second photocopiable, page 113 requires the children to experiment further using a greater variety of line. Ask them to use bold, strong lines, to show a very powerful sea in which the waves are rolling and unfurling, and to contrast these with shorter, thicker lines where the waves have crashed down and broken. Wavy lines can be used to express the tops of the waves. You may find it useful to play appropriate atmospheric music whilst the children work.

The best results will be obtained by encouraging the children to use the photocopiable pages as sketching sheets on which to try out ideas. They can then do their final pictures on larger activity paper, and can introduce colour, working with an appropriate range of pastels.

Here is the start of a picture of a very stormy sea.
▲ Can you finish it by adding lots of swirling angry lines?
You could add a little boat in your picture being tossed about by the huge waves.

EXPLORING MOODS

To develop the ability to express and communicate moods and feelings through drawing.

†† *Whole class, working individually.*

⊕ *45 minutes; follow-up sessions.*

Previous skills/knowledge needed

Mood pictures and story telling can be undertaken with the youngest children and very few previously learned skills are required. Their drawings will however benefit from having undertaken some basic line drawing 'exercises' as outlined in Experimenting with line, page 16 and Making it move on page 18.

Key background information

Young children, prior to developing sound writing skills, express themselves primarily through drawing. They need plenty of opportunities to draw and paint events and experiences that are personal to them. Unlike older children they have no difficulty in recording more than one scene from a story within one picture, or in assembling various related images. By discussing with them how to record a range of moods and giving them opportunities to try out ideas, their ability to express themselves coherently can be greatly enhanced.

These activities are essentially personal and whilst the initial introduction is best undertaken with the whole class or group, make opportunities where possible for the children to develop their drawings quietly without interruption. At times art should be a silent activity.

Preparation

Before the lesson look for a picture in which the artist is depicting a particular mood. There are many Victorian artists whose pictures depict grief, joy or loneliness, but be prepared to show the children examples of more 'difficult' work, for example Picasso's *Weeping Woman*. There are many other Picasso paintings and drawings in which he depicts a strong sense of emotion that the children will find very interesting, and which they will readily be able to describe and discuss. Spend five minutes before the lesson looking very hard at the picture you have selected and prepare a list of questions to ask the children. Remember there are no right and wrong questions to ask the children and nor is it necessary to have any prior knowledge about the picture to be able to lead the class in discussion. Photocopy page 114, one copy per child.

Resources needed

White paper (A5 initially, but later of a size and shape to suit the needs of the activity), sketching or 2B pencils, oil pastels or coloured wax crayons. Photocopiable page 114.

What to do

Begin with some simple exercises. Hand out the drawing materials and ask the children if they can draw a happy line, a sad line, an angry, frightened or worried line? What sort of line would make them feel contented or nervous? Whilst there are no right or wrong answers to these questions they should begin to get the children thinking about using line for expressive purposes.

Introduce the children to the notion of mood in pictures. Ideally it would be very helpful to begin by showing them a

picture such as Picasso's *Weeping Woman*. Let them discuss how an artist portrays strong feelings and emotions. Ask them what sort of lines and colours the artist has used. Do they think the artist feels sorry for the people in the picture? Do they agree with the artist's feelings?

Ask the children to try drawing a picture of a person who is sad. What sort of lines should they use? Suggest that they draw their person long and thin. What background can they add to help to try and tell a story related to this person?

They should now try the reverse, portraying someone who is very happy. Again they should consider the type of lines they use and the shape of the person. This emphasis on mood can now be extended to nervous or frightened people, to bullies or to a person who is extremely angry. Whilst there will be a tendency towards caricature the children will also be required to consider carefully the types of lines and shapes which best suit the emotion.

When the children have undertaken this activity, hand out the photocopiable sheet and ask them to complete the frightening scene.

Suggestion(s) for extension

From drawings of individual people, some children can now develop their work to include a specifically remembered scene or event. Encourage the children to think carefully before beginning, to clarify in their minds what it is they are going to depict. They may need to sketch their ideas first, producing some thumbnail sketches (small drawings about 10cm square). For many young children however the urge to get started is so great that they will want to begin immediately; it can be a mistake to make them discuss for too long when they are eager to begin creating.

Colour is an essential element of mood and emotion. Allow the children to develop these drawings into colour by using either wax crayons or oil pastels. By using crayons or pastels the children will be able to concentrate on their exploration of line and shape and be able to retain these qualities in their final compositions.

Suggestion(s) for support

Where the objective is clear, for example the depiction of a specific mood, then support and guidance from the teacher is appropriate. However when the child is engaged in expressing a personal experience then support needs to be given only where requested. Young children do not suffer from the 'I can't draw' syndrome to the same extent as older children, nevertheless it often hovers close to the surface. When children are engaged in personal drawing, they should be encouraged to work directly and boldly without being unduly concerned as to accuracy.

Assessment opportunities

It is appropriate to evaluate a child's response to a given request, for example where they have been asked to depict a happy person, but less appropriate to hold up a child's personal statement to the whole class for discussion. It is sufficient that you are satisfied that the child worked with full commitment to the task. At times in art it may be that effort is evaluated rather than outcome.

Opportunities for IT

Although some children can find drawing pictures on the computer more challenging the opportunity to use an art package for extending work on mood should not be missed. The ability to 'rub out' mistakes, save work in progress and alter colours enables children to work at a single picture over an extended period and to develop it as their ideas develop.

Display the final set of pictures using multimedia authoring software. Set this up to display each picture in turn with the children's own recorded voices describing the pictures.

Looking at works of art

Picasso is excellent for a consideration of the artist's mood. Similarly Munch's *The Sick Child*, or *The Scream*. Many of the Expressionist artists portray strong feelings in their paintings, perhaps the most famous of these being Van Gogh. Take a look at one of Van Gogh's self portraits to provide the impetus for the children to undertake a line drawing or painting of themselves, in which they attempt to portray a particular mood. Rembrandt is another wonderful artist to explore through his self portraits. Pictures of unbridled happiness are less plentiful! Frans Hals *The Laughing Cavalier* may prove an interesting starting point, although this is not always readily available.

Display ideas

Rather than displaying the children's drawings and paintings on the wall make a book, 'People's Moods', divided into chapters on various moods, for example Happiness, Anger, Sadness and so on. Add poems, descriptions and short stories.

Alternatively choose one mood to display, and discuss with the children how best to support their pictures, for example, what colour background should be used to enhance their pictures of happiness, what objects might accompany their work (streamers, balloons, paper hats), and what poems and writings to include.

Reference to photocopiable sheet

It is important that the children have experimented with making a whole series of lines before completing photocopiable page 114. The objective is to create sinister, threatening lines, which may or may not be related to a specific object. Explain to them that we are often more frightened of the unknown than the known, as for example when watching a film they may already have discovered that they are more frightened before they see 'the monster' than

they are once it has appeared! Ask them to try creating a whole series of scary lines which their friends can then look at and try to explain what they can see.

This activity will work very well in black and white, however, it is also appropriate at a later stage to add colour. Discuss with the children which colours they might use to exaggerate further the mood of their picture. At the conclusion try to find a picture of Munch's *The Scream*, which will give the children a further insight into the work of this very expressionist artist.

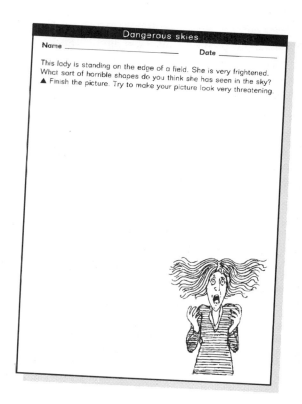

Dangerous skies

Name _____

Date _____

This lady is standing on the edge of a field. She is very frightened. What sort of horrible shapes do you think she has seen in the sky?
▲ Finish the picture. Try to make your picture look very threatening.

FRUITS, VEGETABLES AND PLANTS

To develop the ability to observe, and to record observations accurately.

†† *Whole class or group work.*

🕐 *60 minutes; follow-up sessions.*

Previous skills/knowledge needed

Children at any time during Key Stage 1 could undertake this activity, however it would be appropriate for them to have undertaken some basic drawing skills (see earlier activities in this chapter). Some children will be more adept at recording accurately from direct observation than others but all children need to have regular opportunities to work directly from 'life'.

Key background information

'Good' art work is akin to 'good' science work, and this activity encourages children to explore in considerable detail. It provides the opportunity to consider the structure of a chosen fruit, vegetable or plant, in particular its surface, texture, colour and shape. The initial emphasis should be on very accurate recording through detailed exploration.

Preparation

Decide whether this activity is to be undertaken by the whole class or by a small group. Ensure that there are sufficient fruits, vegetables or plants available so that the children are not working more than four or six to an object. It is important that they are able to observe with ease and to touch the fruit or plant if necessary.

Adequate space is essential if children are to produce interesting drawings. Expecting them to work in conditions where the paper of one child overlaps that of another creates unnecessary complications.

Ensure that any adults helping you are briefed before the activity commences. In particular ensure that they understand the importance of asking questions to encourage the children to look more intently. Whatever the temptations they should not pick up the pencil and do some of the drawing for the children. Make photocopies of page 115 ready for use.

Resources needed

Pencils (2B or sketching), oil pastels, white and coloured paper, magnifying glasses. A selection of appropriate fruit, vegetables or plants (mushrooms, pineapple, onions, red cabbage, peppers, oranges and cheese plants all provide interesting possibilities). Various types of papers, scissors, rollers, press print, printing inks, newspaper and adhesive, paints and brushes, photocopiable page 115, one per child.

What to do

Introduce the activity by handing out the photocopiable sheet and asking the children to complete the cabbage maze! The idea of starting by drawing a very wiggly maze first is useful, as this will give the children the opportunity to 'warm up' before they start the observational drawing. It will also

encourage the children to see the spaces as shapes.

Next, discuss the fruit, vegetable or plant you have chosen for the children to draw. Encourage them to use precise language, for example to describe the surface when explored by touch with their eyes closed, or to explain exactly the colour of the surface. When the children begin to draw they will invariably begin with the outline and then infill the detail. To try a different method ask them to draw the surface they have just described beginning at the centre of the fruit/ vegetable/plant and working towards the edge. Stop them after five or ten minutes and discuss the results with them. Even though they may not have finished move on to the next activity. (It is not always necessary to complete a drawing if the learning objective intended has been achieved; particularly when sketching.)

Ask the children to look at the fruit/vegetable/plant only and not at their piece of paper. They should now start their second drawing. Keep reminding them not to cheat but to look only at the fruit and not at their paper to see where their pencil is going! Again after five to ten minutes stop them and discuss their results. The drawings may look very 'wobbly' but it will have made the children conscious of the need to keep looking at the object they are drawing, rather than working from memory, particularly if they have the object in front of them!

Following this fun activity, allow the children to repeat their drawing, but this time looking both at the object and at their paper. They will now be aware that they should be looking very hard and regularly at the object if they are to produce successful drawings. Again suggest that they begin in the centre of their paper, drawing from the middle of the fruit and working outwards.

With the initial drawings talk to the group a great deal whilst they are drawing, and then on this final exercise leave them to draw una dec. This time they should complete the drawing carefully, and extra time may be required for this.

Further sessions

Further drawings may be attempted at a future stage. Ask the children to undertake a drawing using felt-tipped pens rather than pencils, to avoid the temptation for those who require recourse to an eraser to constantly rub out their drawings. Other media can also be introduced; for example ask them to undertake a drawing using oil pastels, working on grey or black paper.

Develop the theme of line by asking children to select their most interesting drawing or section of a drawing and to redraw it on paper, much enlarged. They should then cut out some of the shapes and stick these onto paper of a different colour. The same exercise may also be undertaken by tearing the paper rather than cutting (this often produces a more lively feel to the work) or by using a wider range of collage materials. The collage may be seen as a finished work or may be used as a block from which to do a print, for example a string and card collage could also be used as a printing

block. Interesting linear prints may also be produced using press print or smooth polystyrene block.

The drawings may also be developed three dimensionally by inviting the children to reproduce their drawings working with papier mâché. If reproducing a pineapple or other 'round' fruit or vegetables use an old ball or balloon as a mould and build up the shell and external texture. Later, when it's dry and the mould has been removed the interior can also be built up, and the whole fruit painted.

Suggestion(s) for extension

Other drawings and studies of sections through the fruit and of small detailed areas may also be attempted. Encourage the children to undertake several drawings on the same piece of paper perhaps adding labels to some of them. Some of the drawings could even be undertaken with the aid of a magnifying glass.

Suggestion(s) for support

Talk regularly to the children during the initial drawing activities pointing out features of the object, encouraging them to draw to the required size, and to work with accuracy and care. Be wary of drawing on their work yourself, but where appropriate stop them and demonstrate on the board or on paper. For example, remind them of the importance of using lines of various thickness and qualities, or of how to produce a particular texture.

Assessment opportunities

Children steadily develop their observational skills during Key Stage 1. Note carefully which stage each child has reached, looking for increased ability to record accurately as they develop their drawing skills. You may wish to record this development by keeping notes, although it is preferable to retain examples of the children's work in order to chart their progress. At the end of all activities evaluate the outcomes with the children, in particular giving them opportunities to discuss the differences between their first drawings and their final attempt, highlighting the improvements and the increasing accuracy of their observations.

Looking at works of art

Cézanne's still lifes (water-colours) are worthy of discussion with the children, as are some of Van Gogh's paintings of flowers (sunflower paintings or pictures of cherry or apple blossom). Georgia O'Keeffe's large semi-abstract flower heads provide an alternative viewpoint. Ask the children about the quality of line and colour, for example: Has the artist used the same colour several times in the picture? Have the objects been outlined or is the line broken?

Botanical drawings from text books are also helpful in showing the children drawing for a different purpose.

Display ideas

Display the original fruit/vegetable/plant with the examples of the children's drawings and oil pastel work. Add brief labels, written by the children, to indicate the task set. Exhibit unfinished studies as well as completed drawings; this will help the children see how a project develops.

Reference to photocopiable sheet

The photocopiable activity on page 115 is a good starting point for this activity, but it could be undertaken at any stage. Cabbages (red cabbages are best) are excellent for drawing, although they are complicated, and you may need to help the children by suggesting that they choose only the most important lines and do not try to draw every one. Keep reminding them to see the cabbage as a maze, which they themselves are trying to find their way round as they undertake their drawings. If the children draw immediately in ink they will not be able to rub out; this can at times (but not always) be a useful restriction making them think and look even more carefully before committing marks to paper.

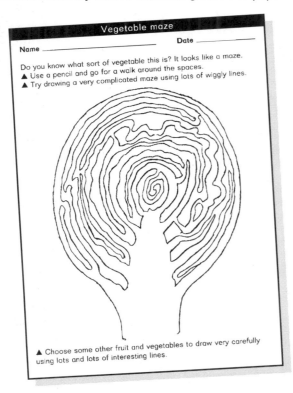

Vegetable maze

Name _____ Date _____

Do you know what sort of vegetable this is? It looks like a maze.
▲ Use a pencil and go for a walk around the spaces.
▲ Try drawing a very complicated maze using lots of wiggly lines.

▲ Choose some other fruit and vegetables to draw very carefully using lots and lots of interesting lines.

EXPLORING STRUCTURE THROUGH LINE

To introduce ways of using line to explain how things work. To learn to be analytical when observing and to record findings using diagrams and drawings.

†† *Small groups or whole class.*

🕐 *60 minutes; follow-up sessions.*

Previous skills/knowledge needed

This activity requires the children to be at a stage where they are able to produce simple diagrammatic drawings. It follows on logically from Fruits, vegetables and plants on page 24 and further develops children's ability to record observations with growing accuracy.

Key background information

As part of the requirements of the National Curriculum you will need to provide opportunities for the children to record what they have observed, to select and sort images and use this source material as a basis for their work. This activity fulfils these requirements and enables you to assess their development.

As well as giving children further opportunities of drawing from direct observation this activity also requires them to consider the design and layout of their drawings. In this the relationship between their drawing and the surrounding space is very important. This is often referred to as positive and negative space. The positive space is the object, the negative space is the area surrounding it. In more successful drawings the negative space is in itself interesting. Thus very small tight drawings surrounded by a mass of uninteresting space tend not to be so interesting to look at, as opposed to drawings where the proportion of positive and negative space is similar. This is one reason why drawings which are 'too big' for the paper and go beyond the edge are often visually interesting because they break up the mass of the negative space. Conversely many children will work on a small scale producing drawings where the space swamps their drawings making even very good drawings look uninteresting.

Preparation

Before beginning this activity look around your school at the drawings on display identifying those which have achieved an interesting balance between the two types of space (remember it may be as a result of the teacher having trimmed the child's work to achieve just this outcome!).

When children are working from observation, from an object or objects in the room, the organisation of the classroom is very important. It is important that all children have a clear view of what they are drawing and that they have sufficient space in which to work. This activity, if undertaken as a whole class activity, demands considerable space. If there is insufficient space in the classroom then arrange to undertake the work in the school hall or other large open space. It's preferable for the children to work on the floor rather than at a cramped desk if their paper is likely to overlap with that of the person sitting next to them. They also need to be able to get up to explore more closely the object they are drawing.

Resources needed

A bicycle (more than one if the whole class is to undertake this activity), white cartridge paper (A5 size for the initial sketches), HB, B or 2B pencils, A4 paper (to draw the whole bicycle). If space is limited draw a group of musical instruments such as a French horn, trombone or other brass instrument, instead.

What to do

Begin by discussing the workings of the bicycle with the children. Ask them to explain to you how the chain, brakes and gears work. Why does the bicycle have spokes? What is it made of? Ask them to select one small section of the bicycle and to look very carefully at how it is made.

Now hand out the A5 paper and some pencils and ask the children to produce a very careful detailed drawing. Once they have finished they can add labels or notes, for example describing the various metals or other materials from which the bike is made. Encourage them to look at and draw not only the more complex sections but also to record a section of the tyre or handle grips showing the pattern.

The children will work at varying speeds, some only producing one or two drawings in the available time whilst others complete four or five. For those finishing first, ask them to take one section of their drawing and to redraw it on a fresh piece of paper. Alternatively they may redraw one of their earlier diagrams. They should now shade their drawing attempting to show the different textures and making their drawings look more solid.

At the end of the session ask some of the children to show their work and to explain to the class what they have discovered.

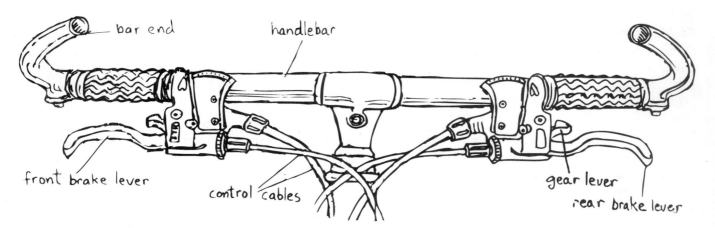

bar end

handlebar

front brake lever

control cables

gear lever

rear brake lever

Further sessions

Now that the children have produced some working drawings, they can undertake a drawing of the whole bicycle during future sessions. Their initial drawings will encourage them to look for detail and will require them to undertake their drawings on a larger scale. Do not worry overly about the scale of their drawings or about their ability to draw perfect circles for the wheels; drawing free-hand circles is an acquired skill that even adults struggle with! Look instead for large drawings that fill the paper and which allow them to show the workings of the bicycle. The children now have a series of drawings from which further art work can be undertaken.

Further sessions on the same theme could include developing line activity based around observations of a bicycle, or might include doing prints of wheels or a weaving using an old bicycle wheel. If the children are going to try some printing, ask them to bring to school a small toy car which they can roll into printing ink and then push across the paper producing tyre tracks. To weave, use an old wheel and a range of wools, cloths and fabrics. Rather than allowing the children free choice ask them to organise the colours so that the dark vibrant colours are at the centre, slowly becoming paler and lighter as they work towards the rim.

Suggestion(s) for extension

More able children will tend to look more closely, working in greater detail. Encourage them to redraw a wheel section including the spokes and then to shade between the spokes trying to produce a variety of tones in the 'negative' spaces. This is a particularly useful exercise for it introduces the children to the notion of positive and negative space. By encouraging the children to shade the space around the bicycle they begin to understand the relationship between the object and its surrounding space.

Suggestion(s) for support

Encourage those children who have difficulty with achieving accurate drawings to run their hands over the section of the bicycle they are drawing then 'draw' in the air tracing out the detail. This will help them sort out the drawing problems before committing lines onto paper.

Assessment opportunities

Whilst the children are undertaking the initial activity observe their ability to concentrate, to record accurately and to add informative labels and notes. In the evaluation at the end of the lesson, note the children's ability to explain their own work and to make suggestions as to how the others' drawings might be improved. When assessing the drawings of the whole bicycle, be prepared to discuss with the children the issue of positive and negative space, in order to help them understand what makes an interesting drawing.

Display ideas

When displaying the children's work avoid cutting around the outside of their bicycle drawings following the contours of their drawing. If the drawings need cutting down, because the negative space swamps their rather small drawings, then retain the original shape of the paper. Where time allows, discuss with the children how much of the original paper should be removed. Their original annotated drawings could also be joined together to form a class sketchbook rather than displayed on the wall.

LINES AROUND THE SCHOOL

To become more aware of the immediate environment, using observations to extend drawing ability.

†† *Small groups; whole class with other adult help.*

🕐 *60 minutes; three follow-up sessions.*

Previous skills/knowledge needed

This builds upon Fruits, vegetables and plants on page 24 and Exploring structure through line on page 26 and is ideal for children who have a developing ability to record accurately.

Key background information

Children require experience of exploring and understanding their immediate environment and this activity provides such an opportunity.

Resources needed

A5 clipboard or similar sized piece of hardboard for each child, white drawing paper, sketching pencil (2B), other coloured papers (black, red, yellow and blue), adhesive, scissors and coloured tissue papers, photocopiable page 116. An example of the work of Mondrian would also be very useful, any of his abstract paintings will be applicable (look in any book on twentieth-century art).

Preparation

Before beginning this activity walk around the school yourself looking for possible interesting areas for the children to draw. Explore both the inside of the building and the exterior.

Identify not only the areas of interest but also any potential difficulties. For example, be clear how the lesson is to be organised: if the whole class is to walk round together stopping at strategic points, ensure that there is sufficient space for them to be able to work in and that they will not disrupt other classes.

Look particularly for interesting windows and doorways, at corridors and stairwells and for good vantage points where large sections of the school can be observed.

Discuss the project fully with the children before they start their journey around the school as it's not always as easy to make teaching points when the class is outside of the classroom.

Photocopy page 116 Through the door, ready for use with the children.

What to do

Use the photocopiable sheet as a teaching aid at the beginning of the task, pointing out how the artist has left out all the small detail and concentrated on the major shapes. Notice also that by looking through a door and then through another door a whole series of shapes within shapes can be seen. Look around your classroom with the children, asking them to identify the various rectangles and squares, for example, windows, doors, tables and cupboards. How many can they identify? In almost every classroom the vast number of rectangles present will readily become apparent and the children will quickly realise that they live in a world dominated by the rectangle.

Give each child a clipboard, some white paper and a sketching pencil. Ask them to do a quick (approximately 10 minutes) drawing of one small area of the classroom in which they look for rectangles within rectangles, such as panels in the door surrounded by the door and the door frame, or perhaps a window with another window or door seen through

it. They may start by drawing a scene with flat shapes seen against a wall, and then, when they have accomplished this, draw a picture similar to the photocopiable, where there is depth to the picture.

Once the class or group have clearly identified what they are looking for take them outside or to other areas of the school to find more examples.

Encourage the children to make their own decisions as to what to draw, undertaking a number of drawings and spending ten to fifteen minutes on each. Their drawings should be linear using a pencil, they need not worry about shading their work at this stage.

Discuss with the children the results of their sketches. Those children who have completed drawings with lots of rectangles in them, are likely to have more interesting compositions than those who have managed to include only two or three.

Further session

During the next session, ask the children to select for themselves the most interesting section from one of their drawings. They may outline the section with a thick dark line so that they can easily identify it as they work. Using a larger piece of white paper as the background, they should now cut out strips of black paper and arrange them on the white background in the same order as their drawing. (See illustration above.) They can select from the red, yellow and blue paper to cut out further rectangles to fill in some of the spaces on their compositions.

At this point, if you have been able to secure an example of the work of Mondrian discuss the picture with the class. They will discover that they have not only completed a delightful picture made up of lines and rectangles but that they have also produced a piece of modern art!

Suggestion(s) for extension

Rather than adding to the background and building up the black lines, ask the children to begin with a sheet of black paper and cut out the rectangles filling in the spaces with coloured tissue paper to create a stained glass window. Alternatively they could use the selected section from their original sketch as the starting point for some pattern work. They should draw the design out again and then experiment by adding twisting, curling lines of varying sorts into each of the 'windows'.

Suggestion(s) for support

Less able children will require guidance in choosing suitable areas to sketch, and may need help in selecting the section of their sketches they use to do the follow-up work. If they find difficulty cutting the black lines be prepared to cut strips for them.

Assessment opportunities

Whilst the children are working, note those who are able to work unaided and make judgements for themselves. At the end of the project discuss with the class the results of their work, considering both which are the most interesting designs and those which show evidence of good technical skills.

Opportunities for IT

Extend the rectangle theme using an art or drawing package. Children could be shown how to draw and position rectangles of different sizes on the screen, and then build up their own pictures or patterns based on rectangular shapes. If the rectangles are filled with different colours children could print these onto an ink-jet OHP transparency sheet and make their own stained glass to display on a window.

Line

Looking at works of art

The work of Mondrian has already been identified as being integral to the development of this project. Browse through any book on twentieth-century art in the library and you will discover pictures by other artists, where rectangles are an important element of their work. Look especially for works by Hockney, Kandinsky, Rothko or other artists of the De Stijl group who worked in the same style as Mondrian. How many rectangles can the children see? Are they all enclosed within the picture frame or do some of them extend beyond the edge of the picture?

Reference to photocopiable sheet

Page 116 shows a scene through a door of a room full of rectangles. Almost any house or room is full of rectangles. For an adult drawing this, with some knowledge of how to represent perspective, it is very difficult not to add triangles too (as in the photocopiable!). For young children however, this does not represent such a problem. Do not, however, expect them to introduce diagonals. For the vast majority of pupils this ability will develop considerably later.

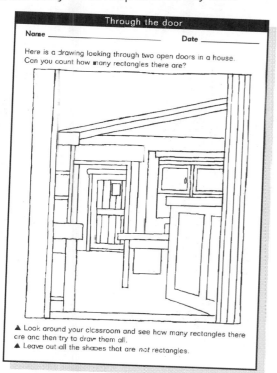

Through the door

Name _____   Date _____

Here is a drawing looking through two open doors in a house. Can you count how many rectangles there are?

▲ Look around your classroom and see how many rectangles there are and then try to draw them all.
▲ Leave out all the shapes that are *not* rectangles.

DRAWING PEOPLE

To develop the use of line through exploring the work of one artist. To understand how artists use line in their paintings.

†† *Whole class or small groups.*

⊕ *Discussion 20 minutes; drawings 2 hours split into sessions.*

Previous skills/knowledge needed

This activity is designed for children who have already experimented with various mark-making activities and who have reached a stage where they can record with some accuracy. Children still drawing symbolically can however still gain much from the activity.

Key background information

This activity is based on the work of Mary Cassatt. Remember that if the whole class are to undertake this activity they are likely to cover a wide range of drawing abilities. Some will be able to record with accuracy and, to an extent, work in the style of Cassatt, but others despite the careful introduction will achieve drawings which bear little resemblance to Cassatt's work or indeed reflect the arrangement of the models! Nevertheless the activity is appropriate for children of all abilities to attempt.

Preparation

Study the poster of *Mother and child* by Mary Cassatt (in the separately available pack accompanying this book) before the lesson, and jot down a few key questions that you are going to ask. These should not only be about the artist's use of line but also might include questions concerning the artist's use of colour, the way in which the figures are posed, the mood expressed and even the relationship between the two figures. Ask questions like: Do you think the artist has finished the picture? Why do they think it was drawn and who do you think it was drawn for? If you are inexperienced at talking about pictures with children remember that there are no right and wrong answers to the questions you ask. Children lack the inhibitions of most adults when discussing works of art and will constantly surprise you with the perceptive comments they make. To help you, a few simple questions are on photocopiable page 145, and some notes about Mary Cassatt and this poster are on page 144.

The activity requires the children to draw one of their classmates sitting holding a large doll on their lap. The child chosen will only be required to pose for ten minutes, returning for brief extra sessions as the need arises whilst the children are drawing. Arrange the room so that all children who are to be involved in the activity will be able to see the model. If it is to be a whole class activity and space is very tight then it may be better to arrange for the activity to take place in the hall or other large space, in which case the children may need to draw while kneeling on the floor.

Photocopy page 117, one for each child, and copies of pages 142 to 145 as appropriate.

Resources needed
Poster of *Mother and child* by Mary Cassatt (in the pack accompanying this book), photocopiable page 117 for the activity, pages 142 and 143 for further work and pages 144 and 145 as background help, sets of oil pastels, grey or other neutral coloured activity paper, further sketching paper if required.

What to do
Display the poster where all the children have a clear view and ask them to look at it in silence for about two minutes. This encourages them to really study the art work, and to realise how important it is to look very carefully. Take the poster down and ask the children to describe what they have been looking at. Can they remember such things as the position of the hands, the colours of the woman's dress and the look in the child's eyes? After their memory has been exhausted replace the poster and allow them to look again. They will now be very keen to explore the poster to check their initial impressions. Introduce a few questions of your own which have been prepared before the lesson (see Preparation section on previous page).

Hand out photocopiable page 117 and ask the children to look at the sheet and to attempt drawing a mother and baby themselves. You will need to decide whether the children will undertake these pictures from memory or whether you will provide a posed model. Drawing from a model aids their understanding and helps them to develop their powers of observation, but it is important that children also have the opportunity to express their own experiences and feelings. Drawing a picture of Mum or Dad and themselves from

memory allows children the opportunity to make very telling comments about their views on relationships within the family. Where this is the case the concern is clearly not the quality of line, or the use of space, but the ability of the child to express themselves fully and clearly. Making comment about these drawings may or may not be appropriate. By experimenting with short, quite quick activities like this at the outset of the work you will encourage the children to give careful consideration to the types of lines they should use, and to be 'loose and free' when drawing.

Now select one of the children to pose for the rest of the children to draw. Give the child a large doll to hold, to take the part of the child in the poster. Pose the child and doll in roughly the same pose as in the poster but don't worry about achieving an exact likeness. It would be too demanding for the child to sit with head turned as in the original! Make sure all children have a reasonable view of the model.

Encourage the group to undertake the drawing working directly onto the paper using the oil pastels without drawing in pencil first. Before they begin their main drawing some children may like to try two or three thumbnail sketches (small

drawings about 10cm square) in which they practise the composition. Remind them to work large, and that in the poster the woman appears too large for the paper. They likewise should try to make the sitter too big for the paper. Children find this very difficult so be prepared that, despite constant prompting, some children will still find that they need to draw the whole of both the sitter and the doll. Constantly remind them that the Cassatt picture is made of many different coloured lines and only blended in one or two places. They should attempt to copy this style.

Throughout the activity urge the children to keep looking. Stop them if necessary from time to time, and ask them to look afresh at the model to check how accurately they have interpreted the pose. It is a good idea to give the children an extra piece of sketching paper which they can use to try things out on, whilst they are working on the main picture. They can also return to their thumbnail sketch technique to experiment with textures for the cloth, skin or hair.

Pages 142 and 143 contain further activities for the children based on Mary Cassatt and the mother and child theme, which can be carried out at any stage of your work.

Suggestion(s) for extension
Encourage the children to look very carefully at the surroundings of the scene and, if they have drawn the figures small, to add a background to their pictures. Alternatively where their drawings do not go to the edge of the paper ask them to create a border using the predominant colours in their pictures, repeating the pattern in the clothing of either the sitter or the doll.

Suggestion(s) for support
Where children fail to record what they see, drawing 'symbolic' representations of the figure, ask them to describe the position of the child posing and how it differs from their own drawing. Having discussed the drawing, ask them if they can make the necessary changes to their own drawing. If they are unable to do this despite your intervention, then leave the child's drawing as it is. Do not do the drawing for them, but accept their drawing for what it is; a record of the child's drawing development at this time.

Assessment opportunities
This activity offers good opportunities to assess the children's progress in recording accurately what they see. By the end of the activity it will be clear that some children will be able to record with considerable accuracy, whilst others may still be at the symbolic stage of development. For those drawing symbolically despite their best endeavours, their drawings will not reflect what they have seen. In these instances the model is unlikely to be sitting on the chair but rather standing with the chair 'wrapped around them'. The arms also may not be holding the doll but rather stuck out on either side of the body. The result may be a charming, rather naive drawing completed to the best of the child's ability. The range of drawings produced will enable a diagnosis of the children's stages of development.

Looking at works of art
There are many other artists who have taken the theme of 'mother and child'. Picasso and Henry Moore in particular are worth researching. Consider asking the children to collect examples from home. These may include Christmas cards of madonna and child, or pictures from calendars or magazines. You could also ask them to bring in photographs of themselves as babies being held by their mothers or fathers. This will encourage further discussion of the various poses found.

Display ideas
Consider displaying the children's finished art work surrounded by their sheets of initial studies. Add a few brief comments about what most interested them in the Cassatt picture. Encourage them to also add a comment about what they were particularly pleased with in their own pictures and display these alongside the artwork and sketches.

Reference to photocopiable sheets

At the beginning of the chapter the children were asked to experiment with using differing types of line to express various moods. Photocopiable page 117 returns to this idea. Photocopiable pages 142 and 143 provide further activities for the children to complete based on the theme of parents and their children. Page 144 provides background information about the artist Mary Cassatt and the poster and page 145 provides some sample questions for you to pose to the children about the poster.

USING LINE IMAGINATIVELY

To develop the ability to use differing qualities of line to express thoughts, feelings and moods.

†† *Small groups or whole class.*

🕐 *Three sessions of 60 minutes each.*

Previous skills/knowledge needed

This activity provides the opportunity for the children to demonstrate their growing ability to use a range of mark making to create lively and interesting pictures. It is most appropriate for children towards the end of Key Stage 1.

Key background information

Children require the opportunity to work imaginatively as well as from observation. Links between art and language should be looked for to help develop discriminative powers. Just as children learn to use precise language to describe feelings so they should learn to use precise lines or colours to express feelings in art.

Preparation

Consider carefully the choice of atmospheric music before beginning, listening to one or two pieces to identify the most appropriate for the class. (*Fingal's Cave* by Mendelssohn, is used as an example but there are other equally applicable works.) Before the lesson ensure that all the materials are available and are easily accessible to the children. Prepare copies of photocopiable page 113.

Resources needed

Soft sketching pencils (2B), cheap sketching or kitchen roll paper, A3 cartridge paper, an assortment of wax crayons, charcoal and chalk, Redimix or powder colour and a full range of brushes, collage making materials and adhesive. Photocopiable page 113. If you are using music (such as *Fingal's Cave* by Mendelssohn) you will need the appropriate tape or CD and a player.

What to do

The theme for this activity is Under the sea, however a number of other titles could easily be used with similar results, such as The jungle, Mysterious world or The enchanted garden which would also allow children opportunities to develop their expressive use of line.

Begin by providing the children with a quite specific stimulus. Ask them to close their eyes, sit quite still, and to imagine a world under the sea. Play the music you have chosen.

Continue by asking them to open their eyes and introducing the children to quite specific words which describe life under the sea: smooth, slippery, darting, curling, twisting, resting, rippling. As you introduce the words ask the children to draw lines on the sketching paper using chalk, charcoal,

Line

and sketching pencils making lines which correspond to the words. They should soon build up a mass of descriptive lines. Encourage them to think before they make their lines, pressing both heavily and softly making thin, thick, jumpy, nervous and bold lines.

Now hand out the photocopiable sheet and ask the children to complete the wave picture. Encourage them to use as many different types of line as possible.

On a second sheet of paper ask the children to begin organising their lines into a composition, drawing on their original attempts and the ideas they explored on the photocopiable activity. Encourage them by telling them to imagine fish swimming – what lines do they make, how is the water moving, what lines would a crab make as it scurries across the sea bed, or plants as they wave within the flow of the water? They should use as many different types of line as possible. At this stage avoid letting them draw the fish or plants, encouraging them to concentrate on capturing the feeling of movement.

Further sessions

Once they have explored the theme, they will be ready in a future session to draw their compositions. To do this they should repeat the lines using wax crayons and washes of paint, building up a 'wax resist' texture to represent the movement of the sea. Once the background is complete, ask the children to add brightly coloured fish and plants. This activity is ideally suited for collage work. The children should consider whether they wish to tear strips of paper and add this to their background as well as cutting or tearing fish and plant shapes. They should also consider adding further textures, by using sponges or card to dab to the surface,

and materials such as lace, polystyrene, bubble wrap, thin netting and sequins are all excellent 'under the sea' materials.

Whilst the children are making their pictures consider playing appropriate music to reinforce their imaginations.

Suggestions for extension

Some of the children could go on to make simple string prints, twisting string onto a glued piece of card to describe the movement of water. When the card is dry the children can print their line patterns onto paper, and fish shapes can then be cut out and printed on top. Using a variety of wools, coloured fabrics, foil, netting and strips of foam, the children can produce weavings on simple card and string looms. If they 'bunch' the thread in places and pull it loose in others they can express the feel of waves, ripples and the motions of water.

Suggestion(s) for support

In the initial stages of the activity constantly talk to the children whilst they are working. Some children may rush their work without giving due regard to the quality of line or the composition. By constantly talking to them, reminding them of the key issues, this problem can largely be overcome.

Explain and help them with techniques, such as differing ways of achieving textures with a sponge, but show them on a piece of scrap paper rather than working directly onto their pictures.

Assessment opportunities

Following the introductory session note how the children are able to differentiate and interpret differing qualities of line

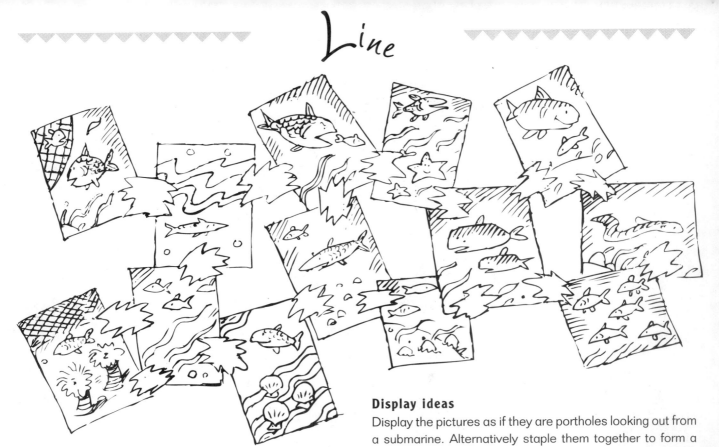

and use them appropriately in their pictures. At the end of the activity, encourage the children to show their pictures to the rest of the class and to talk about particular sections with which they are pleased. It may be necessary to lead any discussion of whole class achievements by asking such questions as: Which pictures do you think have got the most interesting types of line? Who has managed to get a feeling of movement into their work?

Opportunities for IT

The children can experiment with the imaginative use of lines using an art package. Using the freehand drawing tool, with different brushes, pencils and colours, they can draw lines to match the descriptive words. They could then go on to create their own undersea pictures, using the lines with which they have experimented. Avoid using just a fill option to make a background colour, but instead they could use a background colour and put their lines over the top, or simply start with the white screen colour.

The picture could be extended by adding fish, drawn on another screen. These would need to be created, saved and then added to the original background picture. They could then be positioned on the screen, re-sized or altered as the need arose.

Looking at works of art

Paul Klee's paintings The Seafarer, The Goldfish and Warning of the Ships are all excellent starting points for developing further discussion with the class. Alternatively if a book of Klee's work is available introduce the children to his work before beginning the activity. If jungle rather than sea pictures are to be undertaken then the work of Henri Rousseau provides an interesting starting point.

Display ideas

Display the pictures as if they are portholes looking out from a submarine. Alternatively staple them together to form a patchwork of underwater pictures. Try tearing paper to link one painting to another. (See illustration.)

Reference to photocopiable sheet

The Japanese artist, Hokusai produced a wonderful print in which he showed the huge waves towering over boats. The waves were about to break and as they did so they took the form of tiger's claws which made them look even more terrifying. On photocopiable page 113 a wave has been started for the children to complete. Encourage them by asking: How terrifying can you make your picture of the sea?

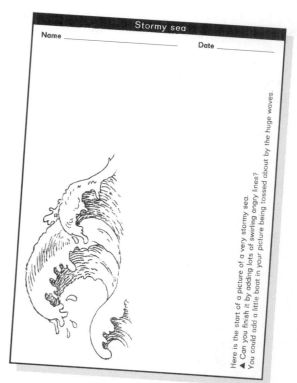

Colour

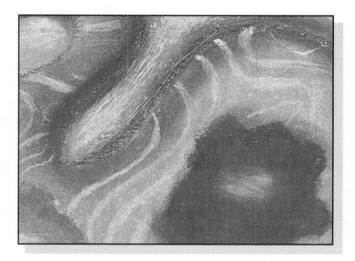

Very young children use colour quite arbitrarily. Given several pots of paint they will move from one to another, over paint, and generally enjoy the physical process of manipulating the paint. As children grow older, colour takes on a symbolic purpose: trees become green, the sky blue and the sun yellow. Only later does the need for more accurate interpretation become important. Children begin to ask the question: 'How do I mix...?'.

Developing the ability to use colour with confidence requires more than the developing of painting skills, and the activities in this chapter also require the children to use pastels, crayons, fabrics and printing inks. The development of painting skills, however, lies at the heart of the chapter. Many children develop a wonderfully intuitive understanding of colour, using it to effect seemingly without any teaching. It is therefore important to provide regular opportunities for the children to use colour freely. Nothing could be more off-putting than to be taught colour through a series of rigid exercises. Nevertheless, children do need to understand the rudiments of colour theory and how to mix specific colours, either when painting from observation or when undertaking an imaginative picture.

Good classroom organisation is essential to support the development of colour work. It is important that the practice of painting is very similar in all classrooms with children required to mix their own paints from the same palette range to ensure continuity and improve confidence.

MIXING COLOURS

To be able to use primary colours to mix a wide range of other colours. To understand the basic processes for mixing colours.

†† *Individual, pairs or small groups.*

🕐 *Two 45-minute sessions.*

Previous skills/knowledge needed

This is an introductory activity for which no previous painting experience is required.

Key background information

Painting is an essential activity in developing children's art, but it can be time consuming to organise, especially if the whole class is to be involved. Nevertheless, children should paint regularly, as the range of brush strokes, textures and the subtlety of colours which can be achieved with paints cannot be reproduced by either crayons or pastels. Many teachers consider they have very limited painting skills themselves. It is therefore good practice to regularly try out the activities before asking the children to undertake the task.

Consider carefully the type of paint which the children are to use. Experiment yourself using both powder colour and 'ready mixed' paints and decide which you think will be the most successful to use with the children. Once this has been decided it is important that all the teachers in the school use the same colours and teach the same procedures. This will help the children make good and appropriate progress with their painting.

The key objective in this activity is for the children to learn the process of colour mixing rather than the achievement of an interesting painting although this may also be an outcome.

Preparation

Prior to the session ensure that the materials required are readily available. Provide an appropriate and consistent range of materials so that the children can learn good practice and

produce interesting and vibrant paintings. Before the lesson spend a few minutes practising using the same materials and colours as the children. This helps ensure that you are clear as to what the children can achieve. Involve any other adults who will be supporting the children at this stage and establish a range of questions to ask the children and decide how much adult involvement will be required. Make sure that there is sufficient space for the children to work freely without getting in each other's way. Photocopy sufficient copies of page 118 ready for the children to use.

Resources needed

Red, yellow, blue, black and white paint. Ideally use powder colour for all painting lessons (except black which is very difficult to mix) although 'ready mixed' in bottle form is also quite acceptable. Two brushes for each child (one small, pointed, one larger with a round end), a cloth or rag for wiping the brushes, flat tray for mixing colours (approximately 15cm × 20cm), white paper, newspaper, and water pots. A copy of photocopiable page 118 for each child.

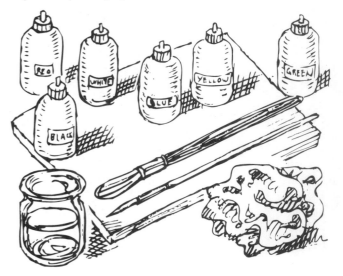

What to do

Begin by asking the children to put small amounts of each of the three primary colours on their mixing trays. Wetting their large brush they should then take a small amount of one of the colours, mix it in the centre of their palette and then paint onto their white paper seeing how far the amount of paint mixed will cover. Allow them to each choose the shape which they paint.

Ask them to take more of the same colour and mix again, this time, however, they should clean their brushes (using the cloth if necessary), and add a second colour to the first, mixing on the palette. This colour should now be applied again seeing how much paper it will cover and again allowing the children to select the shape to be painted for themselves. Using this method the children should now continue with this colour mixing exercise adding more shapes and colours.

Whilst they are working, observe the children closely making sure that they keep their brushes clean when mixing,

only use two colours at a time and paint quite distinct patches on their paper so that they can clearly see the effect of their colour mixing. Ensure they experiment with both brushes.

Introduce the photocopiable page and let the children complete the colour chart using their new skills. At this stage it is sufficient that they should mix equal amounts of each colour when completing the main chart. It is useful however, to get them to try mixing colours in varying amounts in order to understand the effect this has. Learning to take only small amounts of colour is also an important discipline!

Provide sufficient time to experiment with colour mixing, perhaps in a second session, so that they can become familiar with the process without needing to be unduly concerned as to outcome. Give all children the opportunity to follow this activity by undertaking the same process again, but this time working with one primary colour and black and white so that they can discover the range of tones available to them.

Suggestion(s) for extension

Provide more practice with mixing tones of colour. Introduce the notion that they should always start with the light colour and mix the darker colour to it in small amounts. In this way they will quickly learn how to avoid mixing great quantities of unwanted paint.

Suggestion(s) for support

Throughout this activity the children will require constant supervision and support. It is not an activity that can be introduced and then left to continue as a self-maintaining task. Ask the children to identify what happens if they use more yellow or more blue, whether they can remix one of the colours and whether they can forecast a colour before they begin mixing. Children who find this process difficult may also need constant reminders to use their cloths to wipe their brushes or to clean their palette with a paper towel to avoid colours becoming messy.

Assessment opportunities

Closely observe the children working, noting those who are able to mix colours quite independently and making further opportunities for practice for those who are finding it difficult. Discuss with the children their finished work asking them how they mixed certain colours, what areas of their paintings they particularly like or how their paintings using black and white differ from their first pictures.

Opportunities for IT

The children can use a word processor to write and present a label for the display of their work. The time needed for

entering text would be limited and children could focus on formatting their label, selecting and using appropriate fonts and changing its size so that the label can be read across the classroom.

Looking at works of art

A number of twentieth-century artists use colour in an abstract form, Patrick Heron, Kandinsky, Paul Klee, or Delaunay, are all good examples. Look through any books providing a history of art of the twentieth century and you will find appropriate examples to show the children. Ask the children what colours they can see, how many times the artist has used a particular colour and whether they know how a colour has been mixed.

Display ideas

It is valuable to talk about the children's pictures with them. Whilst this is time consuming and cannot be done after every activity, look for opportunities to engage the children in conversation about their work. Brief statements about their paintings can then be displayed next to their work. These statements can be very illuminating and greatly enhance the value of the display. For example, 'I like my painting because it reminds me of...', or, 'I found it quite difficult to...'.

Reference to photocopiable sheet

Photocopiable page 118 provides an opportunity for the children to complete a simple chart in the process of learning how to mix a range of colours.

Colour mix chart

Name _____ Date _____

Mix the colours together to make this chart.

	White	Yellow	Red	Blue	Black
White					
Yellow					
Red					
Blue					
Black					

Now mix red, yellow and blue together in differing quantities. How many different shades can you make?

LEARNING ABOUT COLOUR

To collect, match and identify colours, and to use the outcome to produce colour patterns.

†† *Whole class or small groups.*

🕐 *Three 45-minute sessions.*

Previous skills/knowledge needed

The activity builds on Mixing colours, page 38, and requires the children to mix a range of tones and hues of one colour. They also need to be able to use scissors for cutting out simple shapes.

Key background information

The National Curriculum requires children not only to engage in painting, drawing and modelling, but also to 'select and sort images and artefacts, and use this source material as a basis for their work'. In the painting session of this activity the children are required to further develop their ability to mix colours. For this they will use an extended range of colours, for example, if they are to mix a wide range of reds then they will require two, not one red. In all, they will require a palette which consists of two reds (brilliant and orange red), two blues (dark and blue/green), yellow and white. From time to time they will also need to use black but this should be used sparingly.

Preparation

Ensure that there are sufficient resources for the groups or class, depending on how the activity is to be organised. Brief any other adults who are to help with the session.

Resources needed

Colour magazines, fabric scraps, coloured paper, scissors, adhesive, pencils, paints, brushes, water pots, rags, newspaper and white paper.

What to do

The children should begin by collecting as many examples of one colour as they can. You may decide that the whole class is going to use one particular colour or that each group will collect a different one. Let them look through magazines and cut out any samples they can find. In addition they should look for pieces of fabric and collect tissue, gummed or activity paper of the required colour. When the group has collected a good range the children can then sort them into various colour classifications. For example, if they have been collecting red, they should classify them into bright reds, oranges, purples, pinks and dark reds. Collect and retain their various examples for use later in the activity.

Ask the children to use the paints to mix as many different shades of the chosen colour as possible, working from the palette of colours provided. Let them practise mixing the colours and make a simple chart of all the shades they can

make. Suggest that they start by mixing the lightest colours.

Once these colour experiments are complete, the children can undertake pictures using both the mixed colours and the cut-out pieces. These can either be patterns, for example, starting in the middle of the paper, cutting and sticking on pieces of the very brightest reds and adding some dabs of paint, or they can be used to make imaginary paintings working with such titles as, 'The red landscape' or 'The fiery planet'. Don't make the subject matter too difficult, the emphasis is on colour organisation and too much detail should be avoided.

Best results will normally be achieved where the children keep their pictures 'flat', therefore urge them not to scrunch up paper or stick on balls of paper.

Suggestion(s) for extension

Try making red or blue sketchbooks, sticking two or three very similar reds/blues they have collected onto a page and trying to mix and add a painted square of the same colour next to it. This is quite difficult and therefore appropriate for the more able children.

Suggestion(s) for support

Children will require help with their colour mixing and some will need considerable supervision. Once they start their pictures or patterns stop them from time to time to show examples of good and interesting outcomes. Encourage good craftsmanship, and ensure that they cut out carefully and stick down shapes securely.

Assessment opportunities

Whilst the children are working note those children that are able to use scissors with confidence and are developing their paint-mixing skills. Make brief notes charting the children's progress as they work.

Opportunities for IT

Some children could tackle this work using an art or drawing package. Show them how to select different colours from the full palette or mix their own. They could draw thin rectangle to represent paper strips and fill them with colour, using a roller option. The children will need to remember that if they are using an art or painting package it may not be possible to reposition the strip once it has been drawn. Alternatively children could select a very broad brush and use it to 'paint' strips with the selected colour.

Display ideas

Turn a corner or one wall into a red or blue area. Display the children's work but also exhibit examples of red or blue items, flowers or clothing. Add lists of words that are associated with the colour, or which identify particular hues. The children may also write simple statements about the colour such as 'Red is...' or 'I like red because...'.

FRUIT AND FLOWERS

To accurately record colours from direct observation and to develop colour mixing skills.

†† *Small group (four to eight children).*

🕐 *60 minutes, with further sessions if extension work undertaken.*

Previous skills/knowledge needed

This activity is designed for children who have learned the basic principles of colour mixing. It will be useful if they have completed the previous two activities: Mixing colours, page 38 and Learning about colour, page 40.

Key background information

Regular opportunities for drawing and painting still life are important. Use the activity to introduce more than simply accurate recording. In this instance the children are being asked to consider pattern, space and shape.

The arrangement of the items is important and can either help ensure successful outcomes or create undue problems. It is not sufficient to give the children a bowl of fruit or a plant and ask them to paint it. Consider where the children will be sitting or standing, whether they will have an unobstructed view and what they will see the items against. It is useful to get into the practice of doing this each time you are organising a still life.

Preparation

Before the lesson collect the items the children will be required to draw and paint. Although the children will be helping you select the arrangement of items, set up the background in advance of the session. Place a board as a background to your arrangement and cover two thirds of it with a sheet of yellow paper and the remainder with white. In front of the board place a sheet of blue paper. It will be possible to stand up to four children in front of this arrangement. If more children are to work on this activity at the same time then a further arrangement can be organised on the other side of the board. Remember that if you try drawing the arrangement yourself before the session then you will almost certainly include perspective in your drawing whereas the children will record it as a pattern.

Photocopy page 119 for the children to share working with one page between two.

Resources needed

Background board, sheets of blue, white and yellow paper, a potted plant in a simple terracotta pot and about six oranges, a patterned cloth. Powder or 'ready mixed' paint, mixing palettes, water pots, two brushes per child, rags and newspaper, charcoal, white or buff coloured paper, A4 size. Copies of photocopiable page 119.

What to do

Start the session by handing out copies of the photocopiable sheet and talking together about setting up a still life arrangement. Using the page as inspiration help the children set up their own arrangement. Discuss with them how the objects on the page overlap one another and ask them to look at the space as well as the shapes.

When setting up the still life with the children, try to find an appropriate piece of cloth which has large, simple but bold pattern and arrange a potted plant (terracotta pot) in

Suggestion(s) for extension

In this activity the structure for the still life has been arranged for the children, however, from early on in their art work it is important to get the children used to organising their own arrangements. Give some children items of their own to arrange. Provide some apples, a bowl, and some coloured papers. Ask them to make their arrangement on the floor rather than on the table so that they look down on it when they draw. This will help them to see the pattern qualities.

Suggestion(s) for support

The degree to which you intervene whilst the child is drawing is complex. In this instance be prepared to intervene if a child is producing a drawing which is too small and if the child requires support with mixing colours. However, having carefully organised the activity give the children the opportunity to interpret the still life in their own way. Even an activity as prescribed as this should allow for a variety of outcomes. The best support is often where you regularly ask the children questions, such as 'Can you see the distance between those two objects?' or 'Is that the same colour green as the plant?' In this way children are constantly required to look afresh both at the arrangement and at their own work.

Assessment opportunities

Note the progress each child is making with their colour mixing and also their progress with recording analytically rather than drawing symbolically. Briefly record your observations. Retain their paintings at the end of the session for monitoring progress at a later date.

Opportunities for IT

Concentrate on one particular fruit and use an art package to help focus on the different colour tones. If selecting an apple or banana they can be introduced to different tones or the use of the spray effect to merge different colours together. They need to observe closely and try to match the colours and the way they appear on the fruit.

With more modern computers and software children can often be able to select from a palette of thousands of colours and hundreds of tones of a single colour. You may need to limit this to 64 or 256 to make the task manageable for younger children.

Looking at works of art

Cézanne produced many fascinating still life works most of which are worth looking at with the children. Examples of these are easily available, especially in books on Impressionism or Post-Impressionism. Ask the children to look very carefully at how Cézanne organised the composition. Can they see gaps between some of the objects whilst others overlap? How many colours can they see? Are they bright and colourful or quite subdued?

front of the board and add approximately five or six oranges spacing them so that some are close together and one or two set apart. Let the children contribute ideas on how to place the objects.

Organise the children around the arrangements. Ask them to stand at the tables so that they look down on the still life. Ask them to draw the arrangement using charcoal. Their drawings should fill the paper and it should not be possible to see the edge of the board. Encourage them to draw too large rather than too small. Watch carefully that they fulfil this requirement, asking them to smudge out their drawing with their hand if they work too small and redraw it larger. Ask them to keep looking very closely at the arrangement all the time. Apart from the requirement to draw large and to keep looking, do not interfere with their drawings and allow them to make their own interpretations.

Once they have completed the drawings they should paint them mixing the colours as necessary, for example, mixing green to paint the plant and orange for the fruit. They will also need to decide which of the two blues available best matches the background cloth and similarly which red to use for the pot. This 'simple' still life should however limit the problems of mixing colours. Allow the children to paint the objects in which ever order they wish. If they decide to paint the objects first then add the background later they will 'swirl' around the objects when painting, adding life and vitality to their pictures.

Display ideas

Display the children's paintings alongside the original arrangement. Avoid the temptation to crop their pictures particularly as they have been required to work right to the edge of the paper. If mounting the artwork choose a neutral colour. Too often the qualities of the children's work can be affected or altered by over-bright mounts or backing paper.

Reference to photocopiable sheet

The photocopiable page 119, provides children with the opportunity of seeing how their arrangement might look. It can be used therefore as an introduction to the activity. The main purpose of it is to help the children understand how a very simple still life can be set up which can be both interesting and challenging. You may be tempted to ask the children to colour in the photocopiable page. Should you decide to do this be very clear as to the learning objective, the children need to develop their own drawing skills and to interpret their own ideas rather than relying on the images of adults.

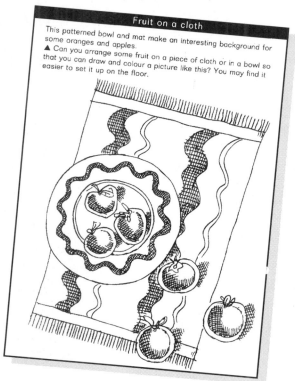

Fruit on a cloth

This patterned bowl and mat make an interesting background for some oranges and apples.
▲ Can you arrange some fruit on a piece of cloth or in a bowl so that you can draw and colour a picture like this? You may find it easier to set it up on the floor.

STORMY SEAS, SUNNY SKIES

To develop the use of colour to express moods and feelings.

†† *Small group or whole class.*

🕐 *Two 45-minute sessions.*

Previous skills/knowledge needed

The activity is designed for children who are able to mix colours with some confidence.

Key background information

The children should be given regular opportunities to explore the potential of paint, working on pictures where the subject matter allows them lots of freedom to experiment. Be prepared to spend some time at the beginning of the session discussing with the children the range of possibilities but once they begin the activity they should be given every opportunity to work unaided.

Preparation

Try one or two experiments before the session, for example, mixing paint with a little PVA adhesive and fine sand to achieve a thick impasto effect, or rubbing the wooden end of the brush into wet paint or dabbing a sponge full of paint onto a dry background. This will help you to be aware of the potential for creating interesting textures and colour combinations as well as anticipating problems which may arise during the session. If the range of materials and processes to be made available to the children is modest then this activity can be undertaken with the whole class, otherwise it may be best to work with a small group. Whichever arrangement is decided upon ensure that all the materials and equipment required are easily accessible.

Whilst it is not essential to show the children examples of famous paintings before beginning and very good results can be achieved without, nevertheless it is very helpful to show children pictures of the sea so as to fire their imagination. While not easy to find, Emil Nolde (look for books on Expressionism) produced some wonderful moody pictures of the sea, and some of The Fauves (early twentieth-century artists) created wonderful hot, sunny paintings of the south of France.

Photocopy page 120 ready for use with the children, one copy per child.

Resources needed

Paint palette consisting of two reds, two blues, yellow, white and black, two brushes for each child (one flat end, one pointed), water pots, rags, mixing tray, newspaper and white or grey paper, PVA adhesive, fine sand and sponges. Aprons for the childen. Copy of the painting *Snowstorm at Sea* by Turner (look in books devoted to Turner's work). Copy of photocopiable page 120 for each child.

What to do

Begin by asking the children to close their eyes and imagine a storm at sea. What would the waves look like, how would the sky appear? Ask them to consider the colours they would see, would the sea be blue and the clouds white? If they wanted the sea to look really frightening how would they show the waves and what colour would the sky be? (If you have collected some pictures of the sea by famous artists show these to the children and ask them whether they think the artist has managed to make a frightening scene.) How could they paint pictures where the sea is really swirling, where you can run your hand over the surface and almost feel the waves? Can they paint a picture where the paint is very thick and lumpy and the colours are really menacing and frightening so that you would not want to go into the water?

Explain to them how they can use not only the paints but may also add adhesive or a little sand to give their pictures more texture. If they wish they can also have a piece of scrap paper to try out textures and colours on before adding them to their pictures. Remind them that they do not have to use the 'correct' colour of sea and sky but should use whichever colours they think will make their pictures look really menacing. Once the children have started, confine support to helping them with the technicalities of mixing, allowing them freedom to interpret the scene in their own way.

If possible allow the children to complete their paintings in one session. It will be useful to discuss the completed work with them, in particular asking them to describe their pictures to their classmates. At this point you may ask them if they wish to make any alterations or additions. If so, make time for those requiring the additional opportunity.

Afterwards, use the photocopiable sheet to reinforce the ideas with which the children have experimented. Let them draw directly on the page to create a picture to represent the weather. Ask them to imagine they are on their bikes and the rain is pouring down and they can hardly open their eyes. If you have a picture of Turner's *Snowstorm at Sea* this will help give them a very good understanding of how their pictures might look! You may decide to use the sheet for the children to complete a sketch and that they then progress from this to undertake a much larger picture using paint, pastels and crayons combined, to get a really interesting texture and quality to their work.

Suggestion(s) for extension

Ask some children to paint an alternative picture of the sea on a very different day. This time ask them to consider they are at sea on a very bright, sunny day, there is no wind at all, the sea shimmers as the sun twinkles on it, there are only a few fluffy clouds in the sky and the land and cliffs they can see in the distance look warm and inviting. What colours do they associate with such a day and what types of brush strokes do they need to make?

Suggestion(s) for support

If the children require help with mixing then be prepared to support by demonstrating, if necessary, on a piece of scrap paper. Encourage those children who require reassurance

ART

by praising their efforts. Ask others to look at their paintings and encourage them to ask themselves if they are pleased with what they are achieving. Can they think of ways they can improve their pictures?

Assessment opportunities

Watch the children carefully whilst they are involved in this activity. Observe their decision making and their ability to experiment. Very often the finished product will not fully reflect the efforts and consideration the child has given to the activity. For example, there may well have been a stage before completion, when the work has looked really interesting yet the child has gone on to overwork the picture. Without intervention very young children will continue working on their pictures until they are virtually black! Continue to keep brief notes on the children in which you identify any significant developments in the child's ability to use paint.

Opportunities for IT

Try using an art package to create pictures of a swirling sea or a threatening sky. This will give the children an opportunity to select their own tones from a palette of different colours and to use different brushes or shape effects to build their picture. Introduce them to the spray effect to help them merge different colours.

Looking at works of art

In addition to the example already highlighted, Munch's *The Scream* is wonderful in its use of threatening colour although it is not a picture of the sea. (Munch is another Expressionist painter and this picture is very widely illustrated.)

Display ideas

Exhibit all their paintings of a storm at sea in one long thin line as if sweeping right along the entire length of the skyline, around your classroom.

Reference to photocopiable sheet

Photocopiable page 120 provides an opportunity for the children to draw an atmospheric scene. Let the children begin by working directly on top of the drawing. They should not attempt to draw in the houses, pavement and road but should concentrate on capturing the feel of swirling, driving rain.

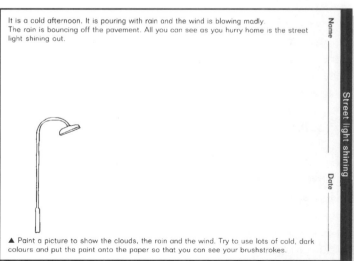

It is a cold afternoon. It is pouring with rain and the wind is blowing madly. The rain is bouncing off the pavement. All you can see as you hurry home is the street light shining out.

Name _____

Street light shining

Date _____

▲ Paint a picture to show the clouds, the rain and the wind. Try to use lots of cold, dark colours and put the paint onto the paper so that you can see your brushstrokes.

46

ART

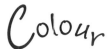

A COLOUR SKETCHBOOK

To increase the range of ways in which colour can be used.

†† *Whole class or small group.*

🕐 *Up to four 45-minute sessions.*

Previous skills/knowledge needed

This activity is designed for children who have a good understanding of colour mixing and who are able to experiment and evaluate outcomes. It is an activity which is best carried out with older KS1 children, who have already had some experience of working with colour.

Key background information

Children are not required to produce sketchbooks until later in their art careers. However, young children are able to experiment from an early age and it is very beneficial for them to keep a record of their experiments, in this instance with paint, in the form of a simple sketchbook. As so often with young children 'good art' is akin to 'good science' and there are many similarities between the two.

A sketchbook does not necessarily mean a bound book or exercise book full of drawings. In this instance it will be a series of experiments on small pieces of paper which can then be put together and a simple cover added. This activity covers many of the requirements of children to be found in the Investigating and Making target of the National Curriculum.

The second session of this activity refers to 'complementary' colour. This is an important concept and young children by the end of KS1 should know that colours opposite each other on the colour wheel, when placed next to each other produce colours which are seen to their fullest intensity. In other words, they complement each other. Find a colour example of the above illustration in an art book to show the children how the colour wheel works.

Preparation

Ensure that the necessary materials and equipment are readily available. If other adults are to work with the children, make sure they are aware of the possible outcomes. Spend a little time with them experimenting before the session or at least show some examples of what can be achieved by the children. This will greatly enhance their ability to support the children. Photocopy page 121 ready for use.

Resources needed

Short strips of card, various small pieces of sponge, feathers, drinking straws, A5-sized paper, wax crayons, pastels, paints, scissors, cocktail sticks, brushes, water, mixing trays, rags, newspaper and other types of paper cut to A5 size, copy of photocopiable page 121 for each child.

What to do

Begin by explaining to the children they are to produce a whole range of painted coloured textures, using many different methods. Carefully save each experiment that the children make and ask them to write one or two words after each attempt, in which they note how they have achieved the effect. The children's experiments should be very carefully undertaken in order to produce worthwhile work.

Provide a range of different types of paper for the children to use and experiment with including brown wrapping paper, newsprint, activity papers and tracing paper as well as better quality art paper. In the first session ask the children to try using items other than a brush to apply paint to the paper. (They may use brushes to mix the paint in their mixing trays first.) They will quickly find that they can use the strips of card to either scrape the paint onto the paper or can dab it on using the edge. Rather than purely making marks on the paper encourage them to produce patterns as they experiment, thus dabbed card lines may be used to make a rhythmical pattern across the paper or scraped colours may be 'spread on' producing wavy patterns across the surface. They should also try using sponges, feathers or blowing paint across the surface using drinking straws to undertake similar experiments.

In the second session the children should experiment using mixed media. In particular they should try using wax or oil crayons and then add quite watery paint over the top to produce a wax resist effect. Show them how to build up the colour with two or three layers using this process. Ask them to note which colours go best together. They should find that complementary colours produce vibrant colours when placed next to each other. When practising with crayons and paints, they should therefore be very careful about the colours they choose to use to produce the best effect. Suggest that they experiment with scratching paint and crayon away to reveal the colour underneath; use the pointed end of a pair of scissors or a cocktail stick to do this.

Join each child's experiments together and ask them to add a cover, to form a sketchbook. The children can use

these to refer to when painting a picture entitled, 'The jungle' or 'The lost planet' or a similar title which will give them the opportunity to use the techniques they have discovered.

As a follow-up to this work, let the children continue developing their skills by using the photocopiable page 121. Working on this activity will develop their ability to mix colour as they will need to find some subtly differing greens to show the wide variations seen in the countryside. If you are fortunate enough to be able to see fields from your classroom window then allow the children to work directly from observation. Otherwise allow them to mix a wide range of greens and either try them out on the picture shown or when designing their own landscape.

Suggestion(s) for extension
Let the children produce their own copy of the colour wheel, and identify examples of the simplest complementary colours. More able children may consider trying to add examples of complementary colours in their final paintings, in order to make their pictures more vibrant and striking.

Suggestion(s) for support
Remind the children of the need to take care with their colour mixing so that experiments are not marred by turgid, messy colours. Although the children are experimenting they should remember that this requires just as much care and attention as when producing a painting.

Assessment opportunities
Look through their sketchbooks and write a brief comment at the end noting how well they have done and highlighting areas they have missed. This will help them realise that sketches and practice sheets can be just as important as a painting or drawing.

Opportunities for IT
The children could tackle one part of this activity using an art package. Compare the differences between using a computer and more traditional methods for this work.

Looking at works of art
A number of art books for children show examples of the artists' sketchbooks as well as of final paintings. The Eyewitness Art books series (published by Dorling Kindersley) is useful in this respect and will help the children realise how even respected artists need to practise and try out ideas before beginning a painting.

Display ideas
Display the children's sketchbooks pinned open on an interesting page with a brief note explaining the children's intentions. This will allow you to show the complete range of their experimentation. The children may refer to these themselves, getting ideas from other children's work as well as their own when undertaking a future piece of work.

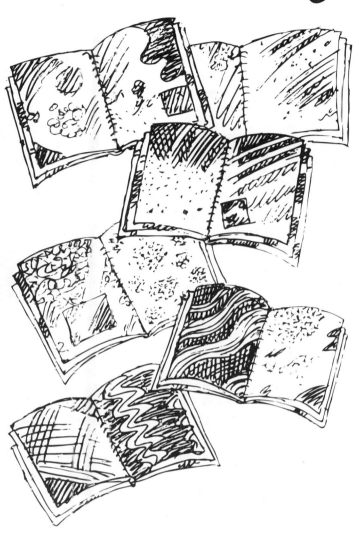

VAN GOGH AND COLOUR

To develop the knowledge and understanding of how a famous artist uses colour and to use this understanding to improve our own painting.

†† *Whole class.*

🕐 *Two 45- to 60-minute sessions.*

Previous skills/knowledge needed

This activity is suitable for children who are able to mix colours with some confidence.

Key background information

This is an important activity for it brings together two skills. From the children's observation of the poster of Van Gogh's *Irises* they will develop their knowledge and understanding of Van Gogh's paintings. They will then be able to use this knowledge and these observations to inform their own painting. In many ways encouraging the children to use their understanding of the work of a famous artist in their own work is a more useful activity than asking them to copy the poster which has a more limited learning outcome.

Be prepared to point out to the children (if they do not tell you first!) the browns, creams and ochre's which Van Gogh uses to depict the soil and the various greens he uses to indicate the rose bush in the background. Point out to the class that Van Gogh does not outline the irises in black and that some of the leaves are outlined in blue. Ask them if they can see any use of black on the painting. This provides a good opportunity to remind the children that often it is best to avoid using black.

Use the picture also to show how an artist often allows objects in the picture to spread over the edge of the paper, indeed some of the irises are cut off giving the impression that the artist has used a camera to zoom in on a small section of the garden. Ask them whether they think Van Gogh was standing or sitting when he painted this picture. Indeed it almost appears as if he was laying down, so tall do the irises appear in the painting.

Be prepared also to discuss the wonderful sense of rhythm in the picture and the long flowing lines of the leaves. There is not a straight line anywhere. Your consideration of the poster will help you to decide how you wish the children to paint their own pictures.

Their enchanted gardens will need to be full of flowers which spread over the edge of the paper and will be made up of many flowing rhythmical lines. They will not find this easy, for young children tend to draw their pictures as if they are hovering above the ground in helicopters!

Preparation

Prior to the lesson spend a few minutes looking at the poster to familiarise yourself with its contents. Note particularly Van Gogh's use of colour and see photocopiable page 149 for

Reference to photocopiable sheet

Photocopiable page 121 shows a sketched scene from a window and asks the children to complete it by mixing shades and depths of green and blues to fill in the detail.

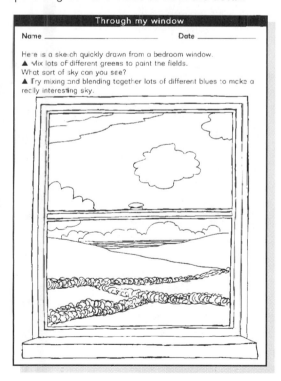

Through my window

Name _____ Date _____

Here is a sketch quickly drawn from a bedroom window.
▲ Mix lots of different greens to paint the fields.
What sort of sky can you see?
▲ Try mixing and blending together lots of different blues to make a really interesting sky.

some key questions to ask (as well as above in 'Key background information') and page 148 provides background information on Van Gogh and the painting itself. Photocopy pages 146 to 149 as appropriate.

Resources needed

Print of Van Gogh's *Irises* (poster in the separately available pack accompanying this book), paints (full palette excluding black), brushes, mixing trays, rags, newspaper, white paper (A3) and pencils or charcoal. Pages 146 to 149.

What to do

Ask the children to look at the poster in silence for a few minutes and then remove it from view. Ask them to describe what they had been looking at. Press them to be as detailed as possible in their descriptions. Refer to the comments in the 'Key background information' (above) asking them, for example, where they thought Van Gogh was when he painted the picture. Replace the poster and discuss with the children the accuracy of their observations and consider further issues about the picture which they have raised. Be prepared to spend some considerable time on this discussion.

Introduce them to the notion of painting a picture of an enchanted garden. Tell them that their garden should be full of huge flowers and like Van Gogh they should be there in the midst of them. Their flowers should be so large that they spread off the edge of the paper. Unlike Van Gogh's garden which was very real and which he was sitting directly in front of, their garden should be imaginary and they can use therefore all sorts of shapes and colours.

Make sure the poster is clearly visible as the children begin work drawing their enchanted gardens. Check that flowers pack the surface of the picture. It may be beneficial to ask the children to try out two or three quick small sketches on a piece of rough paper before beginning.

When the children begin to paint encourage them to apply

the paint thickly in the style of Van Gogh. Once they have mixed a colour they should also look to use it in several places in their pictures rather than painting one small area. In this way they will begin to build up the whole surface of the picture, rather than slowly working across the surface totally completing one small area at a time.

Much can be gained from copying original works of art particularly where the artists' brush strokes can be seen, too often, however we ask the children to work from very small postcards where they can see only the content of the picture and little or nothing of the artist's style or method of working. In these instances the children gain little from the exercise. Use photocopiable page 147 to encourage the children to make a drawing of a single iris. By asking the children to focus on one flower, to magnify the image and then to add paint as accurately as possible, the children are confronted with a range of issues. One of the problems they will encounter is mixing sufficient colour to cover the appropriate area. They will discover that they need to remix accurately when they run out and will see how difficult this can be. Whilst you may encourage them to be as accurate as possible, they will also produce very interesting results as they mix subtly differing blues. The results they achieve may well be quite spectacular!

Using photocopiable page 146 the children can try another flower-drawing task. Try providing the children with a cut flower in tight bud which they can observe and draw over the course of a week as it comes into full flower. Use the photocopiable of the drawings of a daffodil as a way of introducing the idea to the children. They will see that they do not necessarily have to present their drawings linearly but can fill the page so that it appears as a page from a sketchbook. They should concentrate on recording the change of colour as well as the change in form.

Colour

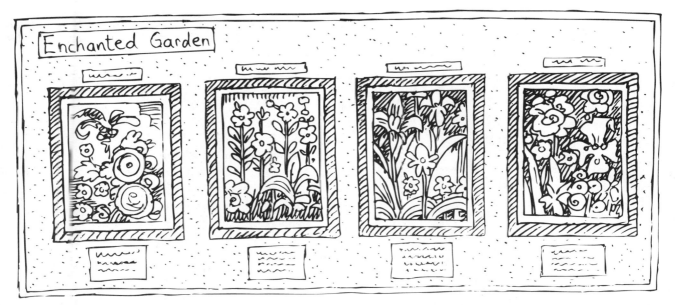

Enchanted Garden

Suggestion(s) for extension

Children showing an aptitude for art should be encouraged to look very closely at the manner in which Van Gogh applies the paint to the surface. Rather than smoothly filling each section as the children will tend to, he makes every brush stroke show. This may look easy but in reality it is very difficult. Nevertheless the more able children should begin to look at mixing colours and applying various blues or greens whilst painting a flower, rather than flatly filling in the area.

Suggestion(s) for support

When sketching out their enchanted gardens, give further support to those children who find difficulty in drawing large flowers which spread beyond the surface of the paper. Do this by referring back to the poster and reminding them how Van Gogh has recorded his garden, but do not resort to drawing it for them. If after further help they are still not able to successfully undertake the task then they should be allowed to do it in their own style.

Assessment opportunities

Add to previous notes where children show an ability to either record with growing accuracy or where the ability to mix paints is significantly improved.

Opportunities for IT

Try using an art package to paint the imaginary gardens, exploring the use of different brushes and effects and selecting from a range of different colours. Large 'blobs' of colour can be created by selecting a very broad brush size and dabbing onto the screen with a single click of the mouse.

Looking at works of art

Camille and the Sunflowers by Laurence Anholt (Frances Lincoln) is a useful book to show the children. It was written from the point of view of a young boy who knew Van Gogh at about the time he produced this painting.

Display ideas

The idea of an enchanted garden has considerable scope for creative writing. Ask the children to write a letter as if from Van Gogh to his brother in which he points out that he has just discovered an amazing garden like nothing he has seen before. They should then go on to describe their gardens. The writing and art work can be displayed together.

Reference to photocopiable sheets

Photocopiable page 146 shows a series of views of a daffodil from bud stage through to full bloom, to inspire the children to make their own series of drawings from a flower. Page 147 is a close-up view of an iris, such as in the original poster, to demonstrate that a close view of a flower can look quite different to the scene at large. Page 148 provides some background information on Van Gogh and the painting *Irises* to help you answer the children's questions and page 149 gives some sample questions which you can ask them.

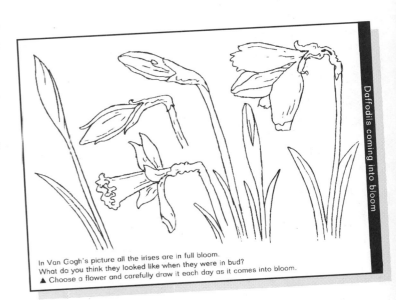

Daffodils coming into bloom

In Van Gogh's picture all the irises are in full bloom.
What do you think they looked like when they were in bud?
▲ Choose a flower and carefully draw it each day as it comes into bloom.

ART

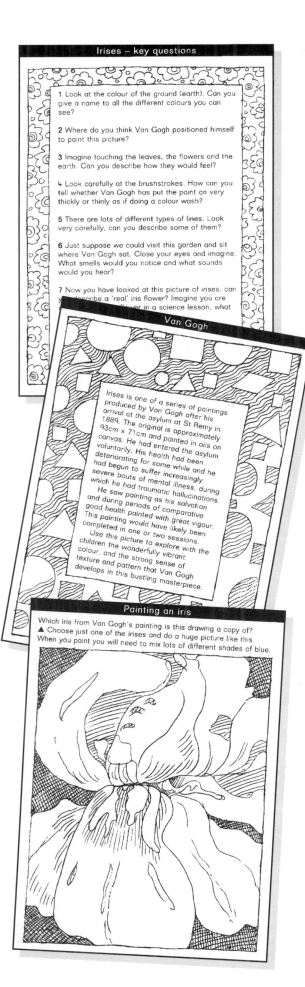

Irises – key questions

1 Look at the colour of the ground (earth). Can you give a name to all the different colours you can see?

2 Where do you think Van Gogh positioned himself to paint this picture?

3 Imagine touching the leaves, the flowers and the earth. Can you describe how they would feel?

4 Look carefully at the brushstrokes. How can you tell whether Van Gogh has put the paint on very thickly or thinly as if doing a colour wash?

5 There are lots of different types of lines. Look very carefully, can you describe some of them?

6 Just suppose we could visit this garden and sit where Van Gogh sat. Close your eyes and imagine. What smells would you notice and what sounds would you hear?

7 Now you have looked at this picture of irises, can you describe a 'real' iris flower? Imagine you are looking at the flower in a science lesson, what

Van Gogh

Irises is one of a series of paintings produced by Van Gogh after his arrival at the asylum at St Remy in 1889. The original is approximately 93cm x 71cm and painted in oils on canvas. He had entered the asylum voluntarily. His health had been deteriorating for some while and he had begun to suffer increasingly severe bouts of mental illness, during which he had traumatic hallucinations. He saw painting as his salvation and during periods of comparative good health painted with great vigour. This painting would have likely been completed in one or two sessions.
Use this picture to explore with the children the wonderfully vibrant colour, and the strong sense of texture and pattern that Van Gogh develops in this bustling masterpiece.

Painting an iris

Which iris from Van Gogh's painting is this drawing a copy of?
▲ Choose just one of the irises and do a huge picture like this. When you paint you will need to mix lots of different shades of blue.

PAINTING DOORS

To understand the importance and value of drawing from direct observation. To use colour creatively in a controlled manner.

†† *Whole class or small group.*

⏲ *One 60- and two 45-minute sessions.*

Previous skills/knowledge needed

The drawing exercise requires the children to have some ability to draw analytically. The colour work in this activity introduces the notion of complementary colour and is designed for children who already have a rudimentary knowledge of primary and secondary colours.

Key background information

By the end of KS1 children should have a good knowledge of basic colour theory which should include those issues undertaken in this activity. This will complete the skills needed for this age group; more advanced work can be left to KS2.

Preparation

If the whole class are to undertake this activity at the same time, then the necessary arrangements for a visit out of school will need to be made well in advance, and you will need to enlist the services of other adults to join your group. Undertake a brief reconnaissance of the area prior to the session yourself, so that you have planned the route and know that there are a good range of doors for the children to draw. Photocopy page 122.

Resources needed

Sketching paper, pencils, clipboards, white paper, paints, mixing trays, rag and brushes (pointed, sizes 6–10), copy of photocopiable page 122 for each child.

What to do

Give each child a small piece of paper. Ask them to close their eyes and to visualise their own front door at home. Can they remember what colour it is? Does it have a window and what size is it? What shape is the door handle? Where is the letter box sited? Is there a number or name attached? Opening their eyes ask how many think they can recall exactly all details of their door. One or two children may then be asked to describe their door to the rest of the class. Following this discussion ask the children to draw their doors on paper. Try this exercise yourself – it is likely that you will have some difficulty remembering all the details, especially if you now try to draw it on paper! Suggest that they take their drawings home and mark them for accuracy themselves.

Following on from these attempts to recall their own front doors, discuss with the children how difficult it is to draw from memory. Point out that where possible they should draw from observation, because their drawings will then have more

detail. Ideally this session should now be undertaken whilst conducting a walk in the local area looking at houses and doors. Take clipboards, A5 paper (which should provide the correct proportions for a door if used portrait style) and pencils and let the children sketch about four or more of the different doors they can see. Ask the children to draw each door on a separate piece of paper filling each sheet with their drawing. They should draw the immediate surround and all the detail they see, but it is not necessary for them to do any shading. If it is not possible to take the children out of school then arrange to take the children on a tour around the inside and outside of the school, and similarly sketch the different doors. If it is not possible to take the children out of the classroom then this project can be done using a wide range of photographs of doors which the children will be able to select from. This is however a poor substitute for drawing from direct observation.

Returning to the classroom they can paint the two most interesting of the doors they have drawn. Before the children start painting, remind them of – or introduce them to – the colour wheel. There is a drawing of a colour wheel on page 47 of this book; you may find it helpful to make a large scale one for use in your classroom to help the children. Simply draw a large circle, divide it into six and paint the sections using the appropriate primary and secondary colours.

The children should not need to redraw their doors. They should paint their first door in tones and hues of one colour, for example if they choose red then they should paint the panels, windows, numbers and frame in varying pinks, plums, oranges and reds. This activity will test the children's ability both to mix colours and also to paint accurately using a pointed brush.

Their second door should then be painted in complementary colours. If their first door has been painted red, then they should paint the second in green. If they have chosen a dark red this should be followed by a light green, and an orange by a bluey-green. Use the colour wheel to ascertain the correct complementary colour. At the end of the painting session each child should have produced two very contrasting doors.

Working from observation of doors will have allowed the children to develop their basic colour understanding. They can now decide on the colours to be used when working on a reasonably simple subject matter. This can be extended by asking them to design, from imagination, a 'simple' pattern on which to work. Many British artists painting in this century have looked at the landscape and tried to break it down into its most essential fundamentals.

Hand out photocopiable page 123. The children may begin by painting this picture, developing their understanding of complementary colours. They can then follow this up by drawing a view out of the classroom window, in which they should try to capture the scene using the very minimum of lines. Again they can choose their own range of colours and not try to recreate the colours they can see.

Suggestion(s) for extension
Develop this idea by encouraging some children to paint a third door in which they use only black, white and greys.

Suggestion(s) for support
When painting some children will need considerable help with understanding how to work out the complementary colour and will need access to a wall chart or drawing on the whiteboard to aid them.

Assessment opportunities
Make notes where relevant of those children who show significant improvement with either colour mixing, painting or drawing accuracy.

Opportunities for IT
Once the children have drawn and painted their doors they could experiment with other doors using an art or drawing package. They could design the outline door, using rectangles and other drawing tools and copy it to make a second door. One could be painted in complementary colours and the other in tones and hues of a single colour. Children will need to understand how to use the roller or fill tool and know that when they are using it the colour will 'leak out' of shapes which are not fully closed. Show them how to use the 'undo' facility so that they can correct any such mistakes!

Looking at works of art
Doors and doorways are fashionable items to photograph. In particular they often feature on postcards and in design magazines. Collect some examples to show to the children to further raise their understanding of the almost endless range of designs within such a seemingly simple object.

Display ideas

Display the finished work in square blocks with groups of 9 or 16 (3 × 3 or 4 × 4) tightly packed together with no space in between. In one panel show all the first doors to be painted and in the other the complementary coloured doors.

Reference to photocopiable sheet

Page 122 shows a simple drawing of boats moored in a port and is a good example of reducing a scene to its most basic elements. It provides an opportunity for the children to use their complementary colour skills. A work by Terry Frost covers a similar theme.

Boats on the sea

Here is a pattern drawn from simple but interesting shapes of boats. The boats are red and orange but the sea is green and blue.
▲ Draw a picture like this and paint it mixing lots of colours.

THE BOX OF MANY COLOURS

To develop the ability to use colour in design.
†† *Small group or whole class.*
🕐 *Three 60-minute sessions.*

Previous skills/knowledge needed

The children will need to be able to cut, stick and organise shapes and patterns.

Key background information

This activity is based on developing the children's ability to design. From time to time the children should undertake art work which has a directly functional outcome; in this it may overlap with technology.

The children will be able to achieve the learning objective without being introduced to the work of any particular artists. However the 'cut out' pictures produced by Henri Matisse towards the end of his life would be ideal to show to them. They are quite easy to research and almost any book on Matisse will have examples of bright, simple, paper collages. If you choose to do this activity based on the children's observations of these works then the children will be able to copy some of the designs, otherwise they will need to make their own shapes and patterns. Both methods are of equal value. You may alternatively use the photocopiable as the starting point from which the children can continue to design their own mythical creatures.

Preparation

Prior to the lesson collect enough small boxes, for example individual cereal boxes or similar, for one per child. Photocopy page 123.

Resources needed

One small cardboard box per child, white paper, scissors, PVA adhesive, a wide range of coloured and shiny papers, pencils and sketching paper. Copy of photocopiable page 123 for each child.

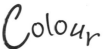

What to do

If you have been able to find examples of Matisse cut outs, start by showing and talking about these with the children. Otherwise, begin by introducing the children to the task – they are to redesign the box creating a design on it which is as bright as possible. Their box should stand out as being very colourful and attractive. It should make anyone observing it want to pick it up before they pick up any other.

Start by covering the boxes in white paper to hide the previous design. Next, work on the photocopiable sheet, adding more creatures to the ones shown. What would they like to draw? Sea horses, sea weed, shell fish, strange deep water fish or fossilised forms? Use the drawings as a catalyst to fire their imagination rather than as shapes to trace and cut out.

The children will now be ready to make some sketches of their own, inspired by the photocopiable activity. These drawings do not need to be neat and accurate but should be a way of trying out ideas quickly, allowing them to reject those which are fussy or uninteresting until they arrive at a design which they like. Discuss with them qualities which make for good design. Shapes should be bold and interesting but not fussy and the negative space between the shapes should be equally as interesting as the positive shapes. (See page 26 for explanation of positive and negative shape.)

Once the design has been broadly chosen they should begin by covering the box with a base colour. This can either be one flat colour or strips or bands of different tones of a colour. Again the children may want to cut the shapes and stick them on or, alternatively, they may try tearing strips

and sticking them on. This method can often produce a more lively and interesting background on which to work.

The children can now design one or two simple shapes which they can cut out and repeat several times before sticking them onto their box to create a loosely repeating pattern. They should ensure that they stick the shapes around the box, with some shapes bending over edges rather than working on one side at a time. Shapes can then be added on other shapes, again not being too precise. The design will be better for being loosely organised rather than rigidly structured for example, working with a ruler to ensure all spaces and shapes are identical. Complete the final design by applying a thin coat of watered down PVA adhesive but warn the children to be careful that this does not cause the dyes in the paper to run.

When the box is complete, line the inside with tissue paper, and add a small weight to keep it upright. Other paper can then be painted with flat colour and spiky or spiralling shapes cut out and arranged to stick out of the top of the box. In this way the box can be completed as if it was a party box with streamers shooting out of the top.

Suggestion(s) for extension

This activity will work equally as well using a cardboard roll as the starting point rather than a box, it could then be designed as a firework in the act of exploding! More able children may develop this project by designing on flat paper being careful with the repeating pattern and then wrapping it around the box once they have completed the design.

Colour

Suggestion(s) for support

Allow the children to choose their own designs but be prepared to offer advice where designs become too fussy and intricate. Give help with cutting and pasting if the children are having trouble with the mechanics of the task.

Assessment opportunities

At the end, assess the outcomes with the children. Ask them: Which one best achieves the objective? Which one is your eye immediately drawn to and which would you like to pick up? This should lead to a discussion about the qualities inherent in good design using their work as the example.

Add to your previous notes where children show a particular aptitude for design work.

Opportunities for IT

The children could use an art or drawing package to create the pattern design for their box. Once they have created one of the pattern shapes for their design, show them how to make copies of this shape and then position the shapes on the background to make a repeating pattern. In some art or drawing packages it is possible to add a background grid so that the children can line up the pattern shapes more accurately. Some art packages have a 'stamp' facility where children can select a pattern shape and simply arrange multiple copies of it anywhere on the screen. Print out the completed patterns, using them to wrap around the box. This is a useful activity to help children appreciate the benefits of using a computer to make an exact repeating pattern.

Looking at works of art

Look at examples of Henri Matisse's, 'cut outs' as described in 'Key background information' on page 54. These bright, simple collages are an ideal stimulus for young children.

Display ideas

Arrange a number of blocks or bricks on a table and cover with a plain white sheet, creating a surface of varying heights. Place the children's decorated boxes on the sheets so that the contents tumble and flow together, yet allowing the box designs to be easily visible.

Reference to photocopiable sheet

Page 123 shows an underwater scene for the children to copy and add to, to act as inspiration for the main activity. Encourage the children to vary the size of their drawings working both large and small.

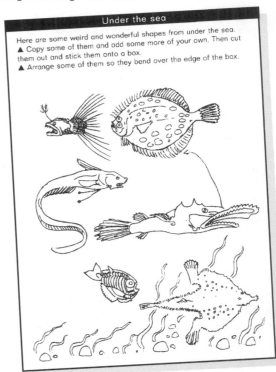

Under the sea

Here are some weird and wonderful shapes from under the sea.
▲ Copy some of them and add some more of your own. Then cut them out and stick them onto a box.
▲ Arrange some of them so they bend over the edge of the box.

ART

Pattern

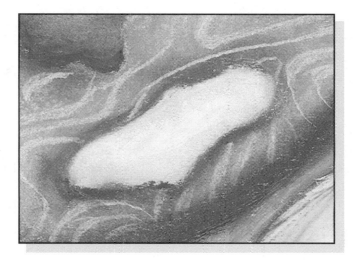

Pattern is inherent in the work of young children. They use increasingly sophisticated shapes arranged across the surface of their drawings to make patterns through which they represent the world in which they live. To begin with these shapes overlap but increasingly as the child develops, the world becomes more organised and the shapes are given spaces of their own. The shapes they produce at this stage create a wonderful sense of pattern which most adults would find hard to copy. It is important that we use these innate talents when planning activities. A number of the activities in this chapter therefore use the children's natural organisation of the picture space to develop activities based on pattern. Pattern is considered in the natural world as well as through using mathematical shapes, letters and abstract shapes. Using the natural world also encourages the child to look closely at their surroundings. Looking is central to most art activities not only in this chapter but throughout the book. Through close inspection of, for example, the fronts of houses in the street in which they live, a bowl of daffodils or the faces of the children in their class, they will develop their understanding of the way in which nature repeats itself in subtly differing ways. By looking for rectangles and squares in the classroom they will also see how some shapes produce quite intricate patterns in ways they had never realised. Through such activities children come to realise that pattern is far more than producing interesting doodles to colour in at leisure.

PATTERN THROUGH PRINTING

To select and organise shapes to make patterns through simple printing processes.

†† *Small group.*

🕐 *Three 30-minute sessions.*

Previous skills/knowledge needed

This is an introductory lesson, the children require no specific previous experience.

Key background information

The activity consists of practical tasks which will give children a clear insight into the basics of making patterns through printing. It encourages the children to experiment with making patterns through using simple printmaking techniques.

Preparation

Ensure that the children have some form of protective clothing available to wear during the lesson. Where helpers are used make sure that they allow the children to do the work themselves and to make their own decisions. Brief any helpers before the session begins. Prepare the materials before the beginning of the session. If you intend using paint rather than a water-based printing ink mix it with a little wallpaper paste to create the right consistency. Have a quick practice yourself with the materials before the session begins. Photocopy page 124 one per child, and page 132 as required.

Resources needed

Newspaper, cheap white paper, either water-based printing inks and small rollers or paint mixed with a little wallpaper paste and sponges. In addition, cotton reels, cogs, small plastic bricks and other similar sized shapes that can be used as printing implements, will be needed in the second session and large leaves or grasses in the third. Photocopiable pages 124 and 132.

What to do

Begin by introducing the children to the notion of pattern by working through photocopiable page 124. Very young children enjoy making patterns, and by asking them to take a line for a walk, thinking carefully about the directions in which it is to travel, and looking at the finished design to see what shapes they have made, you will help them to appreciate some of the characteristics of pattern. Discuss some of the options with the children before they start. Should the line be smooth and bendy or straight and angular? Should it go quickly from side to side or gently meander across the paper? Should they try to watch the shapes they are making to see if they can finish with some large and some small or should they concentrate only on the line and wait to the end to see what they have produced? Let the children have a practice to see what type of line they wish to use before beginning on the photocopied page. When they have completed the page they can colour in the patterns, although it may be advisable, in the interests of time, to select one area to colour rather than attempting to complete the whole design. Follow this up with a class or group discussion on the merits of the various patterns and the children will then have a better understanding of the requirements of pattern making when they start to print.

Begin the printing activity by asking the children to place their hands either into rolled-out ink or into the paint/paste mix, and then pressing them onto paper several times until the image becomes very pale. Discuss the results, identifying which print is the most successful and helping the children discover how much ink they need to use to get good results. Allow them now to experiment placing several hand prints together to form a pattern, placing their prints in a circle, overlapped or interlinked. Tell them to begin using one colour but develop using two or three colours to make the prints more interesting. Towards the end of the session lay the

prints on the floor and discuss the results with the children, asking them which one they like best and why. Consider with them how the prints could be improved if they were to repeat the exercise.

Further sessions

Photocopiable page 132 provides an interesting task, looking at a series of tracks in the snow and requiring the children to make their own print of other man-made and natural objects to make an interesting pattern. Begin with items such as cotton reels, cogs and so on, using the ink or paint/paste as in the first session. After they have made their own patterns encourage them to try again, printing in sequence alternating each item to achieve a symmetrical pattern. They can use a single colour or a selection of two or three colours.

Follow this by asking the children to produce random patterns, encouraging them to decide for themselves where they print the objects on their paper. Again discuss the results with the whole group. Introduce further variations, for example, by asking the children to roll the cotton reel across the surface of the paper.

Suggestion(s) for extension

Children who have completed the tasks successfully might go on to try printing with leaves, flower heads or grasses next. Best results will be achieved by using printing inks and rollers. Ask the children to use a clean roller to roll the leaf onto the paper and urge them to be very careful not to move the leaf whilst they are printing. Develop pattern-making skills by asking the children to arrange the leaves to look as if they are tumbling from the sky or stacked up on the ground.

Suggestion(s) for support

Be prepared to offer technical support, helping children to roll out the ink or to roll it onto the paper if necessary. Ensure,

however, that as soon as possible they do it for themselves. All children should make any design decisions themselves although less able children will need to be supported through careful questioning.

Assessment opportunities

These introductory activities undertaken in small groups will give the opportunity for initial assessment of the children's abilities. They will allow identification of the children's developing dexterity and their ability to select and organise simple patterns.

Display ideas

Ask each child to select the print which they feel is their best attempt. If necessary, discuss with them the need to crop pictures, especially if there are areas which are messy or irrelevant to the main pattern. Display their work with some brief notes as to how they achieved the print. When putting up work of various sizes it is a good idea to begin in the middle of the board and to line up the tops of the prints, working outwards from the centre.

Reference to photocopiable sheets

Photocopiable page 124 invites the children to experiment with pattern, as a useful introduction to the main printing activity. Photocopiable page 132 provides a stimulus for further work on exploring patterns.

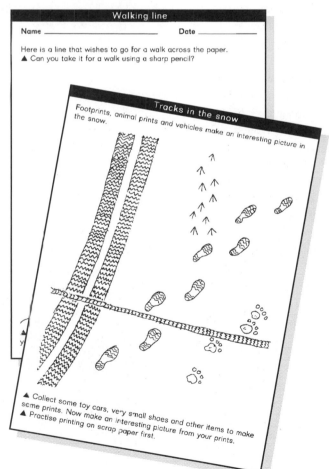

Walking line

Name _____ Date _____

Here is a line that wishes to go for a walk across the paper.
▲ Can you take it for a walk using a sharp pencil?

Tracks in the snow

Footprints, animal prints and vehicles make an interesting picture in the snow.

▲ Collect some toy cars, very small shoes and other items to make some prints. Now make an interesting picture from your prints.
▲ Practise printing on scrap paper first.

LOOKING FOR PATTERNS

To develop the ability to identify simple patterns.

†† *Whole class; small groups for printing work.*

⏱ *Three 60-minute sessions.*

Previous skills/knowledge needed

This is an introductory activity and requires no previous knowledge. To undertake the printing activity, children would benefit from having previously tried some basic printing using their hands and small items such as cotton reels.

Key background information

This activity requires the children to identify pattern within the classroom, to draw some simple patterns themselves and to develop some of their patterns into prints. Give the children the opportunity to look at the work of an artist, such as Matisse, so that they can appreciate how artists use pattern in their own work to express ideas and feelings.

Preparation

Spend a short time before the lesson looking around your own classroom at the wide range of patterns which the children could identify. If other adults are to be involved, make sure they are fully briefed as to their role in the lesson. Look up some examples of paintings by Matisse, for example, *The Red Dining Table*, *Interior with Aubergines*, *The Romanian Blouse*, or any one of a number of his late 'cut outs'. Have these available to look at with the children at the end of the activity. Photocopy page 125, a copy for each child.

Resources needed

White paper (A5), pencils, coloured pencils or crayons, cups and saucers or knives, forks and spoons, teapots, potatoes cut into halves, knives for the children to use, polystyrene tiles (press or easy print), printing ink, rollers, newspaper, copies of photocopiable page 125.

What to do

Start by asking the children to look around the room and to identify the various patterns they can see. They should quickly discover that there are a whole range of patterns, not only on curtains, wallpaper or clothing, but also in the way the books are stacked on the shelves, in the arrangement of

displays on the walls, and in the organisation of tables and chairs. Window panes, panels in doors and indentations in radiators will also provide useful examples of symmetrical patterns. From the children's observations it will be possible to identify with them what a pattern is and just how common patterns are. The children will also be able to see the difference between symmetrical and asymmetrical pattern.

At this point, hand out the photocopiable sheet and ask the children to use it as an inspiration to drawing a pattern of their own. As the children grow more confident in their use of basic shapes to make patterns, introduce them to this idea of using half shapes joined or intertwined together rather than laid out across the surface. Show them how to begin by repeating a simple shape across their paper, for example a square, triangle or simple flower shape. They can try out several different shapes gradually allowing them to become more complex.

Ask them to then select three quite simple shapes which they are able to repeat without difficulty and to draw them, alternating each one, to produce an interesting pattern. They may be arranged in twos or threes across the paper at first, but as they grow in confidence they can begin to consider the pattern vertically as well as horizontally. Colour can also be introduced so that, for example, one shape may be drawn in blue and another in red. The children will begin to realise that it can be quite difficult to continually redraw accurately even a quite simple shape. Suggest therefore that they try printing their shapes to produce a pattern.

Give each child a half or quarter of a potato and knife and ask them to cut their chosen shape into the potato. By dipping their potato into paint they can then repeat print their shape quite easily. They can add other shapes by making further potato cuts.

Once the children have achieved some interesting patterns, develop the activity further by asking them to draw

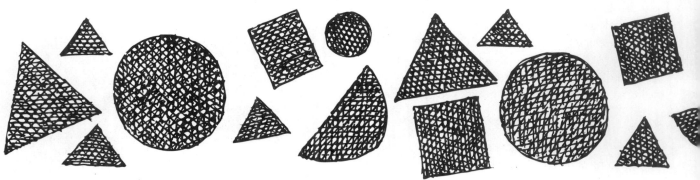

60

ART

some simple observed shapes. A wide range of objects can be used but household items such as cups, saucers and teapots, or knives, forks and spoons will produce the best results. Ask the children to first draw the items onto paper as a silhouette, adding only the most essential detail. They may have to redraw their shapes two or three times until they are satisfied, and they can then take a piece of a polystyrene tile (approximately 8 cm squared) and draw their shape onto it, pressing quite hard to make sufficient indentation on the surface. Make sure they draw the shape as big as possible to fill the tile.

Next show them how to roll out printing ink onto a smooth surface and then by inking up their tile, they can practise printing their shapes onto small pieces of white paper.

Suggestion(s) for extension

Children of differing abilities will produce patterns of varying sophistication. Look out for opportunities to challenge those children who are able to complete the basic pattern drawing task without too much difficulty, encouraging them to try some complex and involved patterns.

These children could also go on to work in a small group of three or four to produce a large-scale joint pattern combining different elements.

Suggestion(s) for support

All children will initially require support when printing for the first time, some will however require close support throughout the whole printing process.

Assessment opportunities

During the activity you will have the opportunity to observe the children's ability to redraw a simple shape accurately, particularly their ability to redraw to the same size. As they develop their patterns some children will see opportunities to produce quite complex patterns whilst others will only recreate simple linear patterns.

When printing observe the children's developing craftsmanship and skills, for example, their ability to work neatly and in an orderly way.

Opportunities for IT

Young children could use framework software such as *My World 2* with a suitable shapes file. They can build up their own simple patterns from the set of pre-drawn shapes provided.

Once they can do this they could use a simple art or drawing package to make up their own patterns from simple geometric shapes. Instead of drawing each shape each time they should be shown how to make copies of a single shape, change its colour and position it on the screen. This activity will lead to useful discussion on the benefits of using IT for this kind of design work.

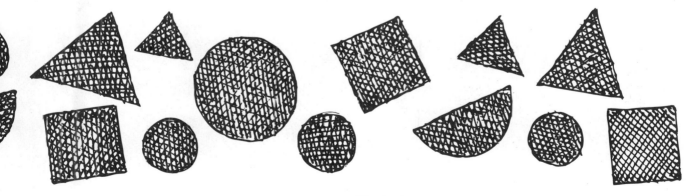

61

Looking at works of art

Many artists use pattern as an important element in their work; Matisse is a particularly good example to show to young children. There are many books showing his work and the examples cited at the beginning of this activity should be easily obtainable. At the end of the activity show the children one or two of his paintings that show bright colourful pattern work. Ask the children to trace one of the shapes in the air. How many times is it repeated, is it outlined, is it an interesting shape and does it go right to the edge and even off the paper? Can the children draw the shape from memory once the picture has been removed?

Display ideas

Display the finished prints alongside the cups, saucers and teapots that the children initially observed. Include some of their original drawings to show the progression. Retain their initial pattern drawings and use these later to provide attractive borders for poems or other creative writing the children undertake and which you would like to display.

Reference to photocopiable sheet

Initially the children may find it difficult to use shapes joined and intertwined rather than simple whole shapes. Photocopiable page 125 will help them to realise the potential for this technique. Having coloured in this example they should be encouraged to try a design of their own. If they struggle to do this, you may decide to give them some templates to help start the process.

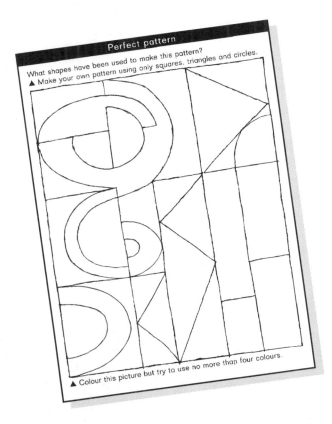

PATTERNS IN BUILDINGS

To develop the ability to see pattern in everyday life.
To develop the ability to select, arrange and organise pattern.

†† *Whole class; working individually and in groups.*
🕐 *Two 45-minute sessions.*

Previous skills/knowledge needed

This activity develops from the previous two activities: Pattern through printing, page 58 and Looking for patterns, page 60. To try this activity the children will need to have had some opportunities for simple pattern making such as printing using their hands or using simple shapes such as cotton reels for repeat patterns. They will need to have looked at patterns around them and be able to identify the different types of patterns. The activity is designed for those children who are beginning to work analytically although children still drawing symbolically will also benefit.

Key background information

This activity develops the children's understanding of the wide range of patterns to be found in buildings. It begins by questioning the way in which they draw houses and through a few selected tasks requires them to draw analytically before selecting and arranging their work in conjunction with other members of the class.

Preparation

Before beginning this activity decide whether the children will base their work on a study of the local environs outside school, the school environment itself or using photographs in the classroom. If you intend the children to make a study of the local environment then you will need to make suitable arrangements to take them out of school, gaining parental permission and organising helpers. You will also need to make an advance trip yourself to take a careful look at the nearby buildings identifying particular features which you will want to bring to the children's attention. If the activity is to be based in school, take a walk around the school observing the various types of doors and windows. If there are problems in taking the children out of school, then take photographs of buildings which they can look at in the classroom. Photocopy page 126.

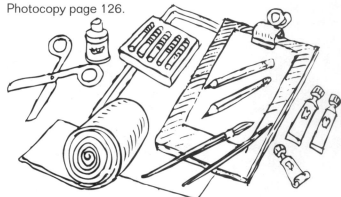

Resources needed

White drawing paper, sketching pencils, clipboards (if the children are to work around the school or in the immediate neighbourhood), crayons, pastels or paints, long strip of frieze paper, a range of papers of differing colours and textures for collage work, adhesive, brushes and scissors. Sufficient copies of photocopiable page 126.

What to do

To introduce this activity there are two alternative starting points. With the first alternative, start by supplying each child with A5-sized paper and a sketching pencil and ask them to draw a house. Don't give any further instructions at this stage. When they have all had a go at this, discuss their drawings with them looking for similarities and differences. Discuss what a 'typical' house looks like, commenting on the variety of windows, chimneys and other features they have included.

Now, ask them to turn their paper over and draw another house this time smaller in size but again in the middle of the paper. This time ask the children to consider carefully the number of windows and doors that they include in their pictures. When they have finished drawing the house ask them to draw a second house next to it. This may be their own house drawn from memory or that of one of their friends or relations.

Alternatively, you may choose to use photocopiable page 126 as the starting point to this activity, encouraging the children to fill their sheets with a variety of houses.

Whichever starting point you have used, continue to discuss house types with the children as they work. Introduce the words: bungalows, flats, detached, semi-detached, terraced and town houses. Talk about houses with lots of chimneys, those with none, the various types of roofs and so on. Be prepared to show them pictures or photographs if you feel this will help their understanding, but at this stage ask the children to work from memory and imagination rather than from direct observation. As the discussion develops they should begin to cover their whole paper with drawings of houses, thereby making an interesting pattern.

Further session

Continue the activity by either taking the children out of school to observe buildings, or by looking around the school. Let the children work with several small sheets of paper attached to a clipboard. Discuss the features of the buildings or doors which the children observe, making them aware of the detail they need to record. Let them make several sketches of different doors or windows.

If working outside is not possible then either supply the children with photographs or ask the children to make a

collection of their own photos of buildings or doors from which they can work.

Returning to the classroom with their sketches, the children can work in groups of three or four and should pool the drawings they have made, selecting the best sketches to work from. Hand out small pieces of paper (approximately 10cm × 8cm) and ask the children to draw and paint the door or building they have chosen, in discussion with their group. Further selections can then be made until the group have sufficient panels to create an interesting pattern. Encourage them to make the final arrangement themselves.

If you haven't used the photocopiable sheet yet, you could finish the activity by handing one copy of it to a small group of children and asking them to make a joint picture. Ask each child to contribute one new building to the scene. Does the final design look muddled if they have all made a contribution? Perhaps it compares well with the town in which they live!

Suggestion(s) for extension

Some children could go on to produce alternative patterns, with the children each drawing a house, tree and vehicle which they 'collage' using a variety of papers and materials. These can then be arranged on a long sheet of frieze paper to produce a whole class pattern of a town. This will work best if the objects are each stuck very closely together.

Assessment opportunities

Assess the children's work against the learning objectives set and look at each child's ability to select and make appropriate choices. Are they able to organise their drawings into an interesting pattern in which there are subtle differences between the objects they have drawn? Look also for evidence of their developing ability to record their observations accurately and to work in a variety of media using appropriate techniques.

Opportunities for IT

The children could use an art or drawing package to draw their house pictures. Make a pattern by importing several of the pictures onto a single screen and arranging them in an interesting way.

Looking at works of art

There are a number of artists whose paintings of houses and buildings have a strong sense of pattern. Perhaps the easiest to research are Lowry (particularly useful to look at with the children if they are to do a frieze of a town), or Hockney (look especially at his paintings of his journeys in California).

Display ideas

As well as displaying their final patterns on the wall, consider also collecting the sketches they have done and making them into a sketchbook. Make a cover and add this to make a 'Sketchbook of Houses'.

Reference to photocopiable sheet

Photocopiable page 126 can be used either as a starting point to the main activity or alternatively as an extension activity where each child is asked to contribute one building to the picture deciding where it should go to make a scene.

Pattern

LOST IN THE FOREST

To create pattern through imaginative drawing. To develop collaborative working.

†† *Whole class.*

🕐 *Four 45- to 60-minute sessions.*

Previous skills/knowledge needed

To undertake this activity, the children require an ability to represent the world symbolically, and also need to be able to produce recognisable forms. It is best suited to children in Year 1.

Key background information

As they develop drawing skills, young children go through a period when they draw symbolic shapes, for example to represent trees. A characteristic of this phase is the tendency to draw each item in the picture as a separate entity. Nothing touches anything else and all things exist in their own space. When drawing at this stage the children create some of the most marvellous design and pattern work. It is an ability that many artists strive hard to reinvent in their own art work but often without success! It is also one of the characteristics which is so enduring in the work of young children, and this activity is designed to exploit this natural talent.

Preparation

Before undertaking the second part of the activity, check that there is sufficient space in the room for the children to do the group work. If not then the groups will need to undertake the activity at different times. As a stimulus you may decide to read a story to the children such as *Hansel and Gretel* (Traditional) or one of the Winnie the Pooh stories by A A Milne (Methuen Children's Books) which will need to be selected before the session.

Resources needed

A4 white paper, drawing pencils and felt-tipped pens or coloured pencils, large sheets of grey or beige paper (A2 size), paints, mixing trays, rags, brushes, scissors and adhesive. A suitable story book (see 'Preparation' above).

What to do

Read your chosen story to the children to set the scene. Now, ask the children to close their eyes and imagine a very beautiful and strange forest full of exotic trees, animals and birds. Ask them to imagine looking down at the ground and to feel and see the plants that live there and then to imagine looking up into the branches to see the leaves and the shapes of the trees. How many different shaped trees are there? How many different types of plants and bushes? Could they describe some of these to the rest of the class? Could they draw a picture in which they show some of these trees, with all their various shapes and forms?

Now ask them to draw the forest on their sheet of A4 paper. While they draw, talk to them, reminding them that no two trees are exactly the same. Make sure that in their pictures all the trees can be seen in all their splendour and encourage them to work until they have filled up the whole of the paper. Within the spaces that are left they may add

ART

one or two of the creatures and birds that live in this forest although if their drawings are already full of interest this may not be necessary.

They are now ready to colour in their scenes. Felt-tipped pens can produce greater vibrancy than coloured pencils. Ask the children to colour in their pictures, reminding them that in this forest everything is full of colour and they do not need to use only green. If there are insufficient pens then either give the children a choice or use coloured pencils. Can they make wonderful patterns on their pictures?

Follow this by arranging the class into groups of four. Each group should then start by drawing, painting and cutting out three or four trees. The children will need to collaborate to check that they do not repeat shapes and as they paint, this time in tones and hues of green, they should ensure that each green is different.

When the trees are complete they can stick them onto the grey or beige paper supplied. Suggest a context in which to work, for example they might produce the Great Wood in which Winnie the Pooh lives, or the wood in which Hansel and Gretel were lost. The task should include producing a maze in which someone or some animal needs to travel as they attempt to find their way. In this way the group can make a pattern of their trees as they stick them down. The inhabitants of their wood or forest can then be drawn, painted and added to complete the scene, at the end of the task.

Sugggestion(s) for extension

Some children could go on to make a monoprint from their initial picture. This requires squeezing out a very small amount of water-based printing ink onto a smooth surface. The ink needs to be rolled so thinly it is virtually dry before they begin. Lay a thin piece of paper over the ink and then place their drawings carefully over the top. (Alternatively they can lay down only their original drawings thereby creating the monoprint on the back.) They should then, pressing quite hard, trace over their drawings. When they lift up the backing paper they will discover a monoprint on the reverse of the paper. If done well these can be delightful, giving the original drawings an interesting texture and adding a real vitality to their work. See page 17 for more advice.

Suggestion(s) for support

The children will all work at different paces and this can be a constant problem, creating timing difficulties for teachers. If some of the children are very slow and do not finish the work in the prescribed time, ask them to select one quite specific area to finish, leaving the remainder as a drawing. By inviting the children used to starting in the middle of their drawings and working towards the edge, unfinished work can look polished, far more so than if the child works from one edge across the paper. Whilst children should always be encouraged to complete their work, even if you have to

provide extra time for them to finish, nevertheless, learning objectives can often be achieved before the natural end of the activity and you may then decide to leave the work unfinished. Make sure however that it is not always the same children that fail to finish the task.

Assessment opportunities
Pin up all their initial drawings, or, if there is not sufficient space then take them into the hall and lay all their drawings on the floor so that they can all observe each other's drawings. Criticising other's work is not easy, even for children, but ask them which they feel is the most successful and why. Ask them to talk about the colours they have used and the patterns produced so that they learn to talk about the visual elements. Add to your individual notes on each child where there has been any significant improvements in the quality of their work.

Opportunities for IT
The children could work with an art package to create their imaginary forest. They will need to know how to select different sized brushes and how to use the spray effect. They will also need to be able to select colours from the palette in order to vary the tones used in the picture. The completed picture can be printed out and then four trees selected and cut out to be used in the group pattern. Compare the computer-drawn trees with the hand-drawn ones and let the children discuss the differences between the two methods.

Looking at works of art
A few 'naive' artists work in a style similar to that used by the children. In particular look at the work of Alfred Wallis, an untaught St Ives painter who produced very interesting pictures of an imaginary Cornish coastline. See *Painting the warmth of the sun* by Tom Cross (West Country Books, Lutterworth) for examples of the St Ives painters. The Tate Gallery at St Ives also produce a useful gallery guide. Discuss with the children how he organises his pictures with houses on their side and villages and boats set out as if drawn onto an old map.

Display ideas
Sometimes the children's work needs to be displayed for teaching purposes as described in the assessment section of this activity. At other times the work should be displayed purely to celebrate achievement. If the work is to be displayed in the classroom then a very simple mount will suffice. If however you wish to display it more prominently, it is worth the trouble of double mounting. Many artists will admit that good framing can considerably enhance even mediocre work and work by children of all abilities will benefit from careful mounting to display in school. It is also worth investing in some 'clip frames' for exhibiting the children's work in the foyer or other prominent areas.

PATTERN THROUGH SHAPES

To identify the wide range of patterns that can be achieved from experimenting with simple mathematical shapes.

†† *Whole class or small group.*

🕐 *Two 60-minute sessions; further time for extension activities.*

Previous skills/knowledge needed
The initial activity requires the children to be able to draw basic geometric shapes. They will need to complete this task successfully to continue to the extension activities.

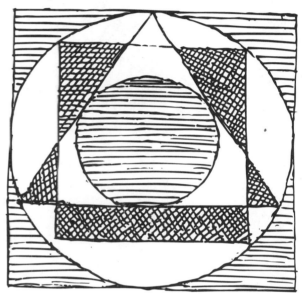

Key background information
Children will be exploring the vast range of patterns that can be made from squares, circles and triangles. It requires them to draw the a variety of shapes and later to develop their work into collage.

Preparation
Collect some examples of the work of Gustav Klimt and select one or two pictures to show to the children before beginning this project. Klimt is a very popular nineteenth/twentieth-century artist and examples of his work are very accessible. Ensure that a sufficiently stimulating range of coloured and textured papers are available before beginning the collage work. Photocopy pages 125 and 127 as required.

Resources needed
Sketching paper (A5), white paper (strong enough to withstand thick covering in point), pencils, red, yellow and blue paint, pointed brushes (approximately size 4–6). A range of colourful papers (coloured foil paper, gummed paper, tissue paper), scissors and adhesive. Illustrations of the work of Klimt, for example *Adele Bloch-Bauer*, *Fulfilment* or *The Kiss*, will add greatly to the activity. Copies of photocopiable pages 125 and 127, one per child.

What to do

Use photocopiable page 125 to introduce the activity, encouraging the children to make a design using a variety of different shapes.

Once they have practised drawing different shapes, ask the children to draw a square, circle and triangle (equilateral) on the sketching paper. They should then practise repeating each shape in a line and keeping to the same size (not getting progressively smaller as they go!). If this is too difficult they may need to draw their own set of shapes which they then cut out and use as templates.

Continue by asking them to draw a large square, approximately 15cm × 15cm, and to fill it with their three shapes to make an interesting pattern. Questions will arise as to whether the shapes should be allowed to overlap, touch, go off the edge of the paper or be in straight lines. Decide with the children what rules need to apply. When the patterns are complete, discuss the results with them, in particular asking what changes they might need to make to produce more interesting results.

Develop the activity further by requesting that they practise putting one shape inside another. They can then try drawing a large triangle and placing a circle inside touching the edges of the triangle. Try the same with a square and a circle, and then a triangle and a square. Again, a square or other simple shape can be filled with shapes within shapes, the children will be learning from the experience of their first attempt. This time ask them to draw their pattern onto the better quality paper so that once completed they will be able to paint their final outcome.

Suggest that they stick to the three primary colours when painting. Again there will be decisions to be made, whether all the triangles should be painted the same colour or whether

they should be varied depending on whether they are large or small. Their patterns should not be too big or contain too many shapes otherwise the children will find the painting task very daunting.

Further sessions

This activity can be extended in future sessions by introducing the children to the spiral, and to 'maze-like' squares and triangles. Ask the children to start in the middle of the triangle and to draw a line coming out so that it ends by describing the shape of a triangle, as shown here. Do the same with a

square and a circle. Now ask the children to produce a new pattern but this one should be much freer, and less mathematical. They may also draw directly in colour using crayons, coloured pencils or paint. They may even wish to consider their designs as a starting point for a fabric design, wallpaper or book cover.

Show the children an example of the work of Gustav Klimt to see how an artist can develop the use of quite simple shapes to produce vibrant, interesting patterns. Discuss with the children how Klimt almost loses the figure amongst the powerful spirals, (see *Adele Bloch-Bauer*). Ask the children what shapes they see, how the artist has organised the pattern, what colours he has used and how they have been arranged, and whether all the shapes are the same size or sizes are varied. Finish by working on photocopiable page 127, letting the children select bright and exotic colours to complete the shape dress.

Suggestion(s) for extension

Some children may now be able to develop their own work in the style of Klimt. Ask them to draw a self-portrait, clothing themselves in a very bright colourful coat with a pattern in the style of Klimt. Rather than painting or colouring they can cut out gummed paper shapes and stick these on to make their patterns.

Suggestion(s) for support

Left to work unaided, some children may produce very small designs, or may start large but then decrease the size of their shapes. Urge them to work boldly and encourage them to consider the spaces left between the shapes.

Assessment opportunities

These activities will allow time for you to observe the children as they work. Their ability to work accurately and neatly will be readily apparent, but time should also be given to discussing with the children their understanding of the issues, for example what they are pleased with in their work or how they might make changes to improve the final outcome. Assess also the children's ability to cut, stick and organise their collage work.

Opportunities for IT

Use drawing or art software to create geometric shapes. Show the children how to duplicate the initial shape to produce mutliples of dentical shapes, which can be moved around the screen, re-sized to make larger or smaller shapes and filled with colour. Make sure that the shapes are completely closed so that the colour does not leak out into the surrounding area.

Display ideas

Be prepared to display unfinished work. This may be work still in progress, to be finished at a later date, or may be left unfinished because the learning objectives have been achieved and to complete further may be a long and unrewarding task. Unfinished work can often show the process more clearly than the finished product.

Reference to photocopiable sheets

There are two photocopiable pages, 125 and 127, which may be used with this activity. You may decide to use page 125 to begin the activity and then move to using page 127 at a later stage (in some of Klimt's work his figures were almost camouflaged against the background, the pattern of the clothes merging with the pattern of the wallpaper).

Again be prepared to use the photocopiable as a quick sketch from which the children can continue to produce their own interesting designs of a person camouflaged against the background.

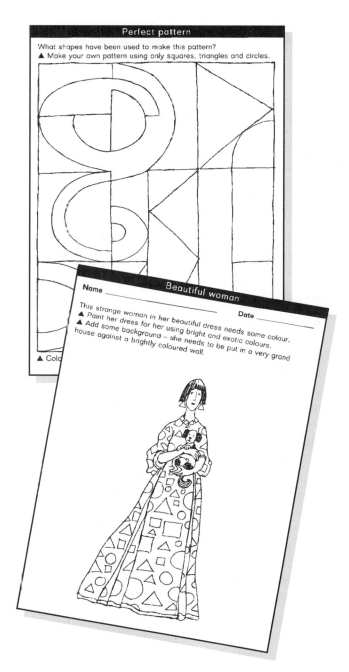

Perfect pattern

What shapes have been used to make this pattern?
▲ Make your own pattern using only squares, triangles and circles.

Name _____ Date _____

Beautiful woman

This strange woman in her beautiful dress needs some colour.
▲ Paint her dress for her using bright and exotic colours.
▲ Add some background – she needs to be put in a very grand house against a brightly coloured wall.

PATTERN IN NATURE

To understand the reoccurrence of pattern in nature.
To develop the ability to observe and record directly
from nature.

†† *Whole class or small groups.*
🕐 *Two sessions of 45 minutes; further sessions for*
design pattern work.

Previous skills/knowledge needed

This activity is designed for children who are able to observe
carefully and record their observations with some accuracy.

Key background information

The children are required to observe in detail a plant or flower,
looking in particular for evidence of pattern in the structure.
They will then be required to develop their drawings to make
their own patterns. A key factor in art work is giving children
the opportunity to come to a better understanding of the
world in which they live. Learning to look very carefully is
essential for the development of children's art work.

Preparation

Choose a plant, flower, fish, insect or vegetable for the
children to work from, ensuring it provides sufficient interest
and detail for the children to be able to extract the necessary
information. If the children are going to work in small groups
with adult helpers, brief the helpers by telling them what you
want the children to achieve. Look for books which show
pattern in nature to provide useful illustrations.

Resources needed

White paper (A4), sketching or 2B pencils, erasers,
magnifying glasses, coloured pencils or water-colour paints
and small brushes (size 2–4), scissors, thin card, printing
inks, rollers, newspaper, and white paper (A3).

What to do

The lesson plan has been based on using a flower such as a
rose, foxglove, bluebell or hollyhock. However, young children
can identify pattern equally as well in a mackerel, pineapple,
cabbage or butterfly.

Choose three or four appropriate plants or flowers. Ask
the children to look very carefully at them, and to look
especially for examples of pattern, allowing time to look and
to discuss any observations. Remember that one of the
reasons for doing art is to come to a better understanding
of the world in which we live and to do this children need to
be taught to look. If, for example, they are looking at a spray
of flower heads on one stem, ask them what similarities they
notice between each one. Are the petals broadly the same
with minute variations? Are some deformed or have been
eaten by an insect? Do the young flowers emerging have
the same characteristics as those lower on the stem?

Following this discussion, ask the children to draw small
sections of the flower in which they attempt to show the
pattern of the leaves, petals or veins on the leaves. Let them
use a magnifying glass if this helps. Allow them to pull off a
flower head, to extract some petals and to draw each one. It
should be possible to cut or pull open the flower head to
observe the stamens inside. By the end of the session they
should have produced a series of almost botanical drawings
through which they will have discovered a great deal about
pattern in nature.

In a follow-up session ask the children to observe a second
flower and compare the two. This time let them use colour
rather than pencil drawing; do not ask them to colour their
original drawings.

Further sessions

From their direct observations the children will now have
some very carefully recorded drawings from which to build
their pattern work. Continue by asking them to copy the
drawing of one of their petals onto a piece of thin card, which
can then be cut out and used as a printing block. Show them
how to ink the 'card petal' using rollers and printing ink and
then print onto paper. Once they have experimented a few
times and have achieved the correct consistency let them
try producing a repeat pattern on A3 paper. This can be done
by alternating the petals up and down, by printing the second
row in the gaps of the first or by printing petals in circles of
four or five. Leaves or stems can then be added using the
same system.

ART

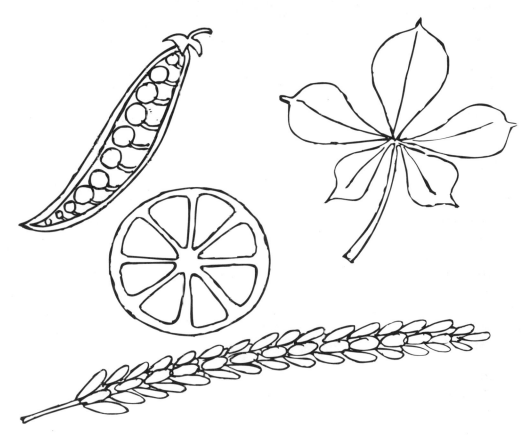

As an alternative to printing allow the children to try drawing around their templates, cutting out the shapes and overlapping them to create shapes within shapes. Again the pattern may be developed on an A3 piece of paper as for a fabric design or alternatively worked up in a long thin strip for a decorative border. Use the pattern for a border design on a book or for a hat band, belt, braces or tie design.

Suggestion(s) for extension

The children may also try the same process using a different stimulus. If the main activity has been based on a flower, look now at a butterfly or piece of fruit and discover pattern in other aspects of nature.

Suggestion(s) for support

Remind the children to think about the quality of their lines. They may need to press harder to describe the edge of the stem than when drawing the softer petals. Hold up and show good examples produced by the children as a stimulus for the rest of the group.

Assessment opportunities

At the end of the task spend some time looking carefully at the children's drawings to identify their progress. Within most classes young children will encompass a wide range of abilities from those who are still drawing symbolically to those who are able to draw quite accurate representations of what they see.

Opportunities for IT

The children could use an art package to begin developing more careful drawing from a section of the flower, a petal or leaf being examples. They will need to have good mouse control skills and be able to select different thickness lines and colours. The completed detailed drawing could be saved and used as the basis for a repeating pattern, or for a border for other work. In many art packages children will need to know how to group parts of their drawing together to form an 'object' which can be copied, re-sized or saved on its own to a disk.

Looking at works of art

Try to find examples of fabrics and wallpapers which show how designers develop designs from their observations of plants and flowers. William Morris is perhaps the most well-known of all designers and examples of his work are readily available. Leonardo da Vinci produced some wonderful drawings of plants which show the rhythms and patterns found in nature.

Display ideas

Arrange a display of the children's work showing examples of the various stages of the work undertaken. Include the original stimulus in the display (such as a vase of the flowers that the children observed or press some of the flowers), and write out a few statements about what the children discovered during their observations and drawings.

PATTERN IN PEOPLE

To identify the wide range of patterns to be found in people and in the clothes they wear.

†† *Whole class or small groups.*

🕐 *60 minutes; three 60-minute follow-up sessions.*

Previous skills/knowledge needed
The activities are aimed at those children who have already undertaken some previous pattern work. It is intended to meet the needs of those children who are beginning to draw with some accuracy.

Key background information
Young children enjoy drawing people, however, as they grow older they increasingly come to the decision that they find figure drawing difficult. By the time they reach secondary school many children will avoid drawing the human figure at all costs! It is important therefore to constantly return to the figure as a subject, giving children a wide range of opportunities to interpret their observations.

Preparation
Ensure that the room is arranged so that all the children can work in comfort and have sufficient space. It is unlikely that the children will produce their best work if their paper is overlapping that of the person sitting next to them. For the second activity you will need an interesting range of patterned materials or items of clothing available for the children to work from: make a collection yourself but also ask the children to bring in examples from home. Photocopy page 128 ready for use.

Resources needed
A4 white paper, sketching pencils (or charcoal), paints and brushes (size 6–8 with a pointed end is likely to ensure good results although some smaller ones may be useful for detail and larger ones for filling in a background wash), a wide range of large-patterned materials and cloths, large sheets of grey or buff activity paper or sugar paper. Examples of work by Picasso or Klee showing the human face. Copy of photocopiable page 128.

What to do
Start by asking one or two of the children to discuss either their father or mother's face. Encourage them to be precise, describing not only the colour of their eyes and hair but also to elaborate on the feel of the skin, the shape of the chin or the wrinkles on the brow! Having described from memory someone not present they can continue by describing themselves or their best friend. The discussion may include some consideration of where precisely the eyes come in relation to the ears or how far down their head they are, but concentrate more on the shape of the eyes or mouth or the

freckles around their nose. In this way you will encourage the children to produce interesting and expressive drawings rather than portraits in which all their efforts have been expended on attempting to get accurate proportions. Such considerations can come later.

Now ask the children to draw the person sitting opposite them on A4 paper. They can take it in turns posing and drawing, until the main features have been recorded. It should be possible for them both to work from this point onwards with quick checks to remind themselves. Tell them to fill the paper with their drawings (they should be drawing head and shoulders only) and check each child's drawing in the first few minutes to ensure they are following your instructions.

Use photocopiable page 128 to give the children the opportunity to work in the same style, either developing further one of the drawings they have already produced or by looking afresh at their friend sitting opposite them. Let them refer back to the photocopiable sheet as they work on their own drawings, or provide an example of Picasso's or Klee's work for reference purposes.

Once the drawing stage is complete ask them to paint their portraits. Again it is important to talk to them whilst they are working, encouraging them to exaggerate any colour they see. For example, Is there any hint of colour under their eyes or in their hair? What colours can they see in the complexion of the person they are observing? The activity gives them every opportunity to experiment with their colour mixing.

When they have finished the head and shoulders ask them to paint in a flat background colour wash. Split the class into four and ask each group to paint their background in a different colour. This will provide a useful tactic when you come to display the children's work!

Further sessions

Develop the idea of 'pattern in people' in future sessions by asking the children to look at patterns in their clothing.

Begin by displaying a range of clothes or fabrics which have interesting patterns and ask the children to select the clothes they are going to dress their imaginary person in.

Next let them draw a 'person' onto paper; if the person is standing then provide a long narrow piece of paper, and then 'dress' the person in the clothes they have chosen by drawing on the appropriate pattern.

Add a background again choosing from some of the patterned fabrics displayed. Their resulting drawings should be a mass of pattern in which the figure is almost camouflaged. Depending on the time available and the complexity of their drawings decide whether the children are to paint or crayon their work; perhaps some children could collage sections of their work.

Pattern and shape are often inextricably linked. This activity can be further extended in future sessions by asking the children to consider the shapes that the human body can make. Take the children into the playground or into the hall and arrange them in a large circle complete with chalk and charcoal and two or three sheets of grey or buff activity or sugar paper. Ask one of the children to pose in the middle of the circle taking up a dance pose, stretching or twisting. The pose should be held for no more than five minutes. Encourage the children to draw the child as large as possible filling their paper.

When three or four drawings have been completed the children should select the one they are most pleased with and ensure it is finished to their satisfaction. Returning to the classroom they can then add paint, working in large vigorous brushstrokes which will add to the feeling of movement. Continue to encourage the children to work quickly, so producing an impression of the figure rather than achieving great detail.

Suggestion(s) for extension

Children who achieve good results with the initial portrait activity could try drawing a group of friends gathered together.

Arrange three or four children with quite different features and see how well the other children can represent their friends! Encourage them to look for as much detail as possible in defining the children's faces. This work may require sensitive handling.

Suggestion(s) for support

The first few minutes of these type of activities are crucial to their success, so it is necessary to walk around giving support and advice.

Assessment opportunities

In each of the activities work closely with the children, constantly talking to them so that they are aware of what is required. Keep looking at their drawings and paintings, assessing their progress and reacting to their needs. For example, if you wish the children to work large and their initial drawings are small then ask them to turn over and start again. At the end of the activity when their work is displayed, evaluate the results with them.

Display ideas

Display is an important element of this activity. When the children have finished their portraits take them into a hall or large space and lay them out in a long line on the floor. Discuss how the portraits could be arranged to form a pattern. For example, they may suggest they are shown boy/ girl/boy/girl, in groups with the same coloured background or as playing cards with the two most similar arranged next to each other. Arrange the 'figure in a dance pose' drawings to create an interesting pattern of swirling movement.

Looking at works of art

Try to obtain a copy of Matisse's painting *Dance* to show the children. This will demonstrate almost exactly the same issues the children have confronted in the final activity. In all work on pattern, paintings by Matisse will provide a very good starting point and his work is very accessible to children.

Reference to photocopiable sheets

Many twentieth-century artists have drawn the human face as a flat pattern with eyes, ears, nose and mouth displayed at odd angles and in unusual places; Picasso is the most well-known. Photocopiable page 128 introduces the children to the notion of the face as a pattern which is then extended into the background. By colouring in the drawing the children will come to better understand the shapes.

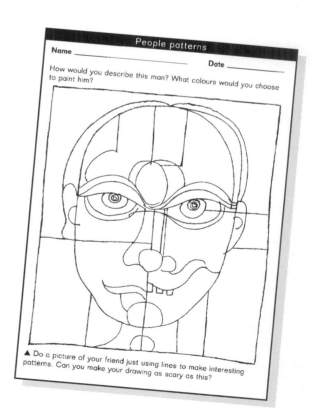

CALLIGRAPHIC PATTERN

To identify the shapes and patterns associated with letter formation, and to explore the potential for art work.

†† *Whole class.*

⏱ *60 minutes; further sessions.*

Previous skills/knowledge needed
This describes an activity for those children who are developing some confidence in their handwriting.

Key background information
This activity, while giving children an opportunity to explore pattern work, also aids their understanding of the variety of shapes within letters. It has benefits therefore as a handwriting exercise.

Preparation
Spend a few minutes practising the activity yourself before the lesson to become familiar with the need to make letter forms touch, and to see the potential of the pattern work. Cut the paper to the correct size before the lesson and have tracing paper available for those children you feel will require some help. Copy photocopiable page 129, one per child.

Resources needed
White paper (A5) folded in half lengthways, small hand mirrors, drawing and coloured pencils, tracing paper, thin card for making templates and further white paper. Copies of photocopiable page 129.

What to do
Introduce the activity by using the photocopiable page. Let the children use mirrors to help them mirror-write the word 'Pattern' on the other half of the sheet.

When they have all had a go at this, ask them to write their own names in capital letters on one side of a folded sheet of A5 paper. Each letter should stretch from the top of the paper to the fold and the letters should touch each other. They should then turn the paper upside down and repeat the exercise making a mirror image of their name. Placing the paper vertically they will see they have created an interesting pattern. If they have not kept each letter to the maximum size and they do not all touch then they will need to rub out and redo their work until they have achieved the desired result. Ask them to look at the spaces and fill with coloured pencils. They may either try to accentuate the symmetry by filling in both sides with the same colour or break up the symmetry by using different colours.

Continue by asking the children to draw three capital letters (perhaps their initials) onto pieces of card approximately 5cm square. Each letter should be about one centimetre wide, and drawn freehand. Again stress the need to fill the whole of

each piece of card. They should then cut out the letters and use them as templates to produce their pattern work.

Rather than having the whole class doing the same activity, this time split the class into two with one half producing patterns from the letters in which each one touches but does not overlap, whilst the other half explore the possibilities from constantly overlapping the letters.

To avoid a great deal of time being spent colouring in their final compositions, ask them to choose just one small area, (no more than 10cm square) and to shade in, achieving as many different tones as they can, using an appropriate 2B or sketching pencil.

Suggestion(s) for extension
The most able will be able to complete the mirror writing unaided. Extend these children by asking them to repeat the activity, but this time using a flowing cursive style. They will find this more difficult although the results may well be more interesting. Help them choose words (other than their own names) which contain no letters with tails, as this will unnecessarily complicate the task.

Suggestion(s) for support
Check as the children are drawing that they are all working to the correct size. Some children will need to use tracing paper in order to obtain good results. Stop the class from time to time, pointing out examples where children are achieving particularly interesting results.

Assessment opportunities

Craftsmanship is a key factor in art work and opportunities should be looked for to see this attribute in the children's work. In this instance the best results will be achieved by those children who have worked neatly and cleanly. Look also for good control of the pencil and the ability to form accurate letters.

Opportunities for IT

The children could use an art or drawing package to extend this work. They could type in their starting word, select an appropriate font, and then enlarge it so that it fills the top half of the screen. Children can then be shown how to duplicate the word and then flip the second word so that it appears upside down. The word can then be positioned so that it touches the first one. The children can then use other drawing and colouring tools to add colour to the pattern which they have made.

Alternatively, children could use the software to create a template letter, which they duplicate and arrange to make their pattern. If the children just add colour to a small section of their pattern they can then copy this across the whole screen to make an identical repeating pattern.

Looking at works of art

An American artist, Jasper Johns, created a number of paintings in which he used letters or numbers as the starting point for his work. Examples of his work are often to be found in books on twentieth-century art, or more specifically in books on modern American art. Some research is worthwhile for the children will readily see close connections between their work and Johns'.

Display ideas

Teachers often give titles to exhibitions of children's art and these are often produced by drawing around templates of letters, cutting them out and pinning or sticking them onto backing paper. Using this method, give the letters to a small group of the children to produce the titles for the exhibition. They should consider mirror writing, overlapping or pattern making to achieve the desired effect.

Reference to photocopiable sheet

Be prepared to give the children tracing paper to start with when using photocopiable page 129, so that they can achieve an accurate copy. Later they can then try working 'freehand'. Alternatively they may cut out the letters and use them as templates to create an interesting design where each of the letters partially overlaps.

Texture

In addition to traditional art techniques, children need the opportunity to develop a wide range of craft skills. Creating a whole series of differing textures using a wide range of materials introduces children to some simple craft activities. It allows them to try out a number of processes and to obtain as much satisfaction from the making of art as in achieving an outcome.

As they develop the skills necessary to weave a wall hanging, create a papier mâché mask or create a collage from which to print, children learn the attributes necessary to become good craftspeople. Where the craft work is poor, for example the weave is left too loose, or the papier mâché or collage is applied with insufficient adhesive, then the final quality of the work will suffer. Young children require help and support to develop good craftsmanship, and when undertaking many of these activities there are opportunities for the teacher to demonstrate, evaluate, explain and encourage in order that the children learn the basic craft skills.

Good art and craft often instils in the onlooker the desire to touch and children in particular require opportunities to touch and handle objects and art works in order to improve their understanding. Alongside looking and listening this is another way in which children come to better understand the world in which they live. Opportunities therefore to explore through touching as well as through creating texture is an important component of many of these activities.

FEELING AND DRAWING

To understand the importance of texture in producing art work.

👫 *Whole class or small group.*

🕐 *Two 45- to 60-minute sessions.*

Previous skills/knowledge needed

There are no specific skills required as this is a session which introduces young children to texture.

Key background information

Texture is an important visual element, as important as line or colour. Children need opportunities to practise and develop their skills in order to be able to include textural qualities in their work. The vast majority of paintings between the Renaissance and the twentieth century appear smooth and highly glossed, and texture does not appear to be an important issue for the artist. However, during the twentieth century many artists have produced paintings in which it is possible to observe almost every brushstroke. Collage, mixed media art work, textile weavings and prints have become an important part of the artist's repertoire, all of which rely heavily on the quality of the texture to provide their effect.

One of the qualities not only of sculpture but also of painting, is the need in the viewer to touch as well as to observe. When visiting art galleries this is seldom allowed and even when touching bronzes the viewer is required to don a pair of soft gloves. Yet to touch art work and to be able to run your hand over the surface can greatly enhance the appreciation of the work.

Preparation

Prior to the lesson prepare bags each containing one textured item (feathers, pebbles, synthetic furs and so on). Provide enough individual bags for the children to have one each and preferably a few spare so that children who work quickly are not held up. Number all the bags. If you have a large group you can duplicate the contents in some. Use any suitable bag or box into which the children can put their hand without being able to see in.

Brief any adult helpers and remind them that they should be prepared to help the children by asking them relevant questions when assisting with a process or technique. They should ensure they do not work on the child's drawings nor criticise their attempts unless they are clear that insufficient attention and care is being taken.

Photocopy page 130 to provide for one per child.

Resources needed

Items such as feathers, sponge, conker shells, glasspaper, pebbles, synthetic fur, scrunched tin foil and so on. Paper bags/cloth bags/small boxes with an opening for a child's hand, charcoal or soft pencils, wax crayons, paint and brushes, small and large (A3) sheets of drawing paper. Copies of photocopiable page 130.

What to do

Ask one of the children to put their hand into one of the bags and describe to the rest of the class what the contents feel like without identifying what they think the item is. Encourage them to be precise in their language. Continue by asking the whole group to attempt to draw the texture from the description they have heard. Allow the child who has described the item to look at the drawings to see which one they feel best matches their description.

Once they have understood the task give each child a bag and ask them to feel the contents and to draw the texture they feel. Tell them to number their drawings according to the number on the bag so that at the end of the session comparisons can be made as to the way in which they have each interpreted the different textures. There should be time for each child to try five or six bags.

Continue by giving each child a large piece of paper (approximately A3) and asking them to draw a range of textures from various stimulus words given to them. Use words such as: spiky, rough, slimy, prickly, gungy and so on. These may either be read to them slowly, giving them time between each word to undertake a drawing, or a series of words shared with them which they can work through in their own time. They should find that the children quickly fill their paper with textures producing patterns in which the textures merge into one another.

Use the photocopiable sheet to support this activity, either introducing it at the beginning of the children's work or later on towards the end of the activity. Ask the children to discuss the textured drawings and see if they can think of other ways they can produce the same textures, improving or exaggerating them further.

Suggestion(s) for extension
Some children may like to try using coloured wax crayons rather than charcoal or soft pencils for the A3 sheet activity. They could then add a colour wash over the top allowing the paint to run off the waxed areas. Encourage them to experiment for themselves producing colourful textures on small pieces of paper which could be used for an abstract card design.

Suggestion(s) for support
Some children may find this task difficult, so be prepared to support them as necessary. They may well need reassurance that there are no right and wrong answers to this task, and that as long as they are thinking carefully and trying their best to produce accurate interpretations, then their work is both valid and appropriate.

Assessment opportunities
Look for development both in the children's use of precise language and appropriate visual interpretations. Keep notes on individual children where you feel there has been significant development. Similarly where a child is anxious or tentative about their art work then a note should also be kept.

Opportunities for IT
The children could explore the idea of textures using the different drawing tools in an art package. Experiment with thick or thin lines, different brush thickness and using the spray can, to create lines with different textures – by moving the spray can more slowly the line becomes thicker.

Ask the children if they can create textures similar to wax crayon or charcoal. Some software even allows children to mix their own colour patterns which can add a different texture to the colour. The final work could be printed out and displayed so that other children can see what kind of effects can be created.

Looking at works of art
Use the Van Gogh poster *Irises*, in the separately available pack accompanying this book, to explore textures created by brushstrokes. What words can the children think of to describe the textures in this painting? If they look very closely can they see the individual brushstrokes that the artist has used? Look around the school for any examples of 'original' art, including that done by the children, where there is evidence of texture being a key component of the work and discuss the work with the children.

Display ideas
From their first attempts at recording textures cut out small rectangles and stick these closely together to create a small textural mural of their work. Display examples of their textured drawings with the bags underneath and invite other children to feel inside the bags to guess which of the drawings matches the bag.

Reference to photocopiable sheet
You may use the photocopiable page 130 at the beginning or end of the activity. It is designed to reinforce the drawings which the children produce from feeling the various textures.

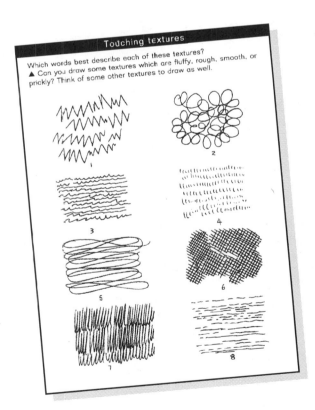

RUBBINGS AND PRINTS

To identify some of the wide range of textures in the natural and man-made world, and to be able to develop art work from these observations.

†† *Small group or whole class.*

🕐 *Three or four 45- to 60-minute sessions.*

Previous skills/knowledge needed

This activity builds on the children's understanding of texture gained from the activity, Feeling and drawing on page78.

Key background information

This activity includes many necessary aspects of an art scheme of work. The children have the opportunity to record from direct observation, experiment with tools and techniques and also with visual elements. It allows them to collect information, make selections and develop technical skills.

Preparation

Walk around the outside of the school building and the playground prior to the session in order to ascertain the potential for rubbings. You should be able to find a wealth of textures. Try doing a few rubbings yourself, as what looks like a good example can often prove difficult, whilst other areas that may look less promising can be very interesting. If there is a church and graveyard or other interesting old building close by you may decide to take the children further afield. If it is not possible to take the children out of the classroom, arrange a collection of items in the classroom from which the children can work. Ideally it is, however, far better that they should explore the environment for themselves choosing their own textures.

Resources needed

Plenty of small sheets of cheap white paper, stubby wax crayons, Plasticine, clipboards, water-based printing inks, rollers, flat trays for rolling out the ink, larger white paper (up to A3), grey or black paper.

What to do

Take the children for a walk around the playground and the outside of the building. Point out to them areas where there are interesting textures. Encourage them also to look for themselves, and to point out places where they think it would be good to take a rubbing. Allow them sufficient time to do five or six different rubbings, giving help where necessary. Make sure that all the children have collected a sufficient range of textures. In addition give each child two small pieces of Plasticine sufficient to produce slabs approximately 10cm square. Ask them to press the pieces onto a part of the building, playground or tree which will give them an interesting indentation of the surface. They should return to the classroom with their rubbings and indented Plasticine.

The children now have two activities to undertake. They will be able to work with their rubbings with little support, however, the printing is a more technically demanding activity and will require some adult support.

They should tear their rubbings into long strips, and stick the strips in layers onto a piece of grey or black paper. Begin with the 'heaviest' rubbings at the bottom of the sheet and work upwards to the 'lightest', to create a section as though through the earth or as if creating a lunar landscape. If they stop about half to two thirds of the way up the paper then a round 'moon' can be cut out and added.

Using their Plasticine imprints they can produce a series of prints. Squeeze a small amount of water-based ink onto

a tray and roll it out thinly using a roller. The inked-up roller should now be carefully rolled across the surface of the Plasticine and then the Plasticine can be pressed firmly onto a sheet of white paper.

The children need to learn to press sufficiently hard to get a good print but not so hard that they destroy the imprint. They should repeat this procedure several times, using the same colour, until they have partially covered the paper. They can then use their second print and a second colour to finish covering the paper. Allow the prints to overlap as this will enhance the quality of their final design.

To finish, hand out photocopiable page 131 and ask the children what the rubbing reminds them of. Could they use it as a starting point for a picture or draw over the top adding lines and further shading? Alternatively they may wish to cut part of it out, stick this onto a larger piece of paper and extend the lines and shading to make a 'new' picture. They can look at their own rubbings to see if they can turn any of these into a picture.

The other photocopiable page 132, shows a series of tracks in the snow and encourages children to make their own picture. Encourage them to collect their own objects that will make interesting textures when printed and to practise printing these.

Suggestion(s) for extension

Encourage the more able children to select a small area of their final Plasticine print which they feel is the most interesting and draw a rectangle around it. They should cut this out and make a simple mount for it.

Suggestion(s) for support

Be prepared to help some of the children with the selection of areas to rub. They may also need support with holding the paper steady.

When printing for the first time ensure that the children do not squeeze too much ink into the tray. They will also need some support with rolling out the ink and applying appropriate pressure in order to get a good print. Do not do it for them!

Assessment opportunities

Make a brief note on those children who are able to make decisions for themselves and show an ability to work independently. Similarly, identify children who require reassurance before they will commit themselves to paper.

Looking at works of art

Max Ernst, a surrealist painter, created a whole series of collages in the 1920s and 30s very much along the same lines as the work produced by the children in this activity. Examples of his work are not, however, easily found and you will need to find a book specifically on Ernst to show these to the class.

Display ideas

Where space is tight consider joining the children's mounted 'landscapes' together concertina style so that they unfold tumbling from floor to ceiling as shown in this illustration.

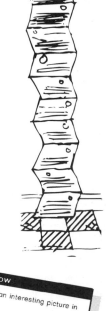

Reference to photocopiable sheets

Photocopiable page 131 is intended to develop the idea of looking at a randomly produced texture in nature and looking for hidden shapes and symbols. Page 132 refers back to work undertaken in the 'Pattern' chapter. In this instance, however, the emphasis is on looking at texture.

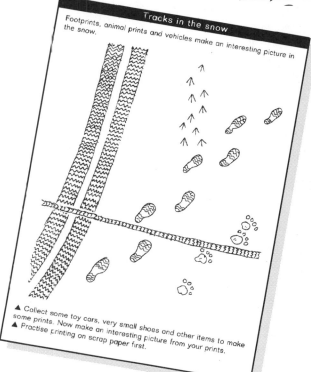

Tracks in the snow

Footprints, animal prints and vehicles make an interesting picture in the snow.

▲ Collect some toy cars, very small shoes and other items to make some prints. Now make an interesting picture from your prints.
▲ Practise printing on scrap paper first.

This is a rubbing from an old wooden beam. Can you imagine a pirate ship being rushed along in a violent storm when you look at this print?
▲ Do some rubbings of other textures and then make them into pictures of fields, skies or swirling seas.

Make a rubbing

A CLOSE-UP ON TREES

To identify the wide range of textures in the bark from trees. To develop an understanding of simple processes involved in working with clay.

†† *Small group.*

🕐 *Two 60-minute sessions.*

Previous skills/knowledge needed

This is an introduction to working with clay and can be undertaken with young children.

Key background information

Clay is a very versatile medium and all children should be given regular opportunities to use it. It is not the only medium however, and Plasticine and salt dough are perfectly acceptable alternatives.

Preparation

Collect a range of differing types of tree bark (hand size or slightly larger) before the session. Take care not to damage any trees when you are collecting bark, only removing pieces which have broken off already. It will be helpful if you can identify the type of tree from which the bark has come so that you can share this information with the group. Brief any adults helping you in the session. Photocopy page 133 ready for use and collect pieces of lace or paper doilies.

Using clay

To get the best from clay observe a few simple rules. If clay is too wet then the children will find it sticks to their hands and to the table and is difficult to manipulate; if it is too dry then it will crack as the children use it and they will become frustrated. It is best therefore to use 'fresh' clay direct from the bag. Keep unused clay constantly covered in a polythene bag to avoid it drying out.

Hold and handle the clay as little as possible. Let the children feel it, pull it and squeeze it for a few minutes to get the feel of it. Give them another piece of clay to work with and ensure they leave it on the table holding it only when necessary.

Use a piece of sacking or hessian for each child to roll out their clay on, to prevent it sticking to the table top. When they roll the clay they should turn the piece of clay over after each two or three rolls; this makes the task very much easier and again stops the clay from sticking.

Make sure that there is an appropriate range of tools available for the children to work with and sufficient for the size of the group.

It is not necessary to fire the children's clay work at the end of the session but if you do have access to a kiln it is worth using. Firing greatly enhances the work and will allow it to be painted using either paint or felt-tipped pens.

Resources needed

Pieces of bark, reference book on trees, a sack of clay, squares of hessian, clay knives, rulers, rolling pins, modelling tools and cocktail sticks, stiff brushes, forks, sponges and sieves, loop cutters, rulers and bowls of water. Photocopiable pages 133 and 134 if required.

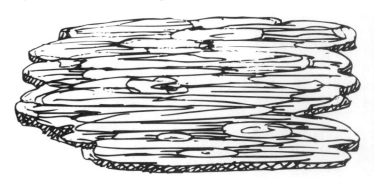

What to do

Ask the children to describe the texture of the bark of a tree. Do they know what colour it is, how many different types there are, and what its function is? Give each child a piece of bark and ask them to explore it with their eyes closed and describe how it feels. If you know which tree each piece has come from, you can then tell the children and you may also have pictures of the trees to show them in a reference book.

Give each child a small piece of clay and if they have not used clay before allow them a few minutes to play with it, exploring its properties. Follow by giving them another piece of clay to roll out into a flat slab. Demonstrate first, showing them how to lightly roll, turning the clay over after each two or three rolls and then ask them to do the same. Once their

Suggestion(s) for support
Be prepared to help the children with rolling and cutting. Once they have begun to work on their textures they should be able to work unaided.

Assessment opportunities
Look for and make notes if appropriate indicating the child's developing dexterity with using tools. Note also where any child begins to show an aptitude for working with clay that has not been obvious in their other art work.

Display ideas
Consider making (or get help to make) a simple, large wooden tray consisting of four strips of softwood attached to a hardboard base. The children's clay panels can then be laid (or stuck if they have been fired) into it to create a large class mural.

Reference to photocopiable sheets
Photocopiable page 133 provides an alternative to working with tree bark. The activity can be developed by cutting up lace to create a collage of a magical garden or a lunar landscape. If the children wish they can take a print from their final picture. This idea is further extended in photocopiable page 134, The scary desert.

clay is rolled out they can then choose two pieces of bark to press into the clay. Having achieved an interesting texture they can cut around the clay using a knife and ruler to trim off the uneven edges. With very young children it is not necessary for them to measure and cut, although with older children cutting two equal-sized rectangles will look better.

Develop the activity by giving each child another piece of clay and asking them to roll out as before. Working from one of their imprinted slabs they should attempt to copy the texture using the modelling tools and cutters. Encourage them to cut into the clay and to build it up, adding textures using stiff brushes, forks, sponges or sieves. They should experiment to see how many different types of textures they can produce. When finished they can again cut round their designs.

Photocopiable page 133 provides an alternative to working with tree bark using old lace or paper doilies to make a magic garden that can be pressed into clay. This idea can be used at any suitable point in the activity to develop the children's skills. Photocopiable page 134 can also be used to provide a further alternative.

Suggestion(s) for extension
If the children show an aptitude and interest for clay work the activity can be extended by asking them to roll out a slightly longer rectangle onto which they draw three or four wavy lines. Working between these lines they should 'texturise' alternative bands, contrasting the rough and smooth elements. When finished stand the clay up on its longest side and bend it round until the two ends are touching to create a cylinder. Join the two ends together using a modelling tool and leave to dry.

The scary desert
▲ Collect a range of interesting things which you can use to make a collage with lots of textures.
What sort of shapes and textures will you use?
You could call your picture 'The scary desert'.

A magic garden
Here is a design for a paper doily.

▲ Collect some old pieces of lace or paper doilies and cut them up.
▲ Arrange them on paper to make a picture of a magical garden.

CATS, PINEAPPLES AND ROCKS

To develop the ability to represent texture using a range of media and working from direct observations.

†† *Whole class for first task; small group for second, if space is limited.*

🕐 *Two 60-minute sessions.*

Previous skills/knowledge needed

This activity requires careful observation. Children should have tried some previous texture work and they should have developing confidence with recording from direct observation.

Key background information

Children (and adults) have a tendency to draw by starting with the outside shape and then in-filling. This activity encourages children to work in the opposite way. Drawings produced by the children can also be of a consistently uniform size, especially if the children are always given paper of the same shape and size. The two tasks in this activity require the children to work both large and small.

Preparation

Cut sufficient 'windows' for the class before the session; use activity paper or thin card and cut a window of approximately 15cm square, framed by a border not less than 5cm wide.

Select the objects or animals the children are going to draw. Provide such items as pineapples, cabbages, cauliflowers, bark, small pieces of rock, a stuffed bird or animal or even a live cat or dog as long as it is docile! If an animal is to be drawn then at least half the class should draw this whilst the remainder work with fruit or vegetables, stuffed animal or bird. If only inanimate objects are to be drawn then the objects can be placed on tables for a group to work from.

Resources needed

Objects or animals to be drawn (rough stones or rocks, pineapples, cauliflowers or cabbages, stuffed animals or birds, cat, dog or other docile animal with its owner), white paper (A4), grey paper (A2), a card or thick paper 'window' (see 'Preparation' above), sticky tape, felt-tipped pens, coloured pencils, soft drawing pencils, oil pastels, wax crayons, chalk and charcoal, paints for a wash, fixative spray, a variety of collage materials.

What to do

Begin by introducing the children to the task and to the objects. Ask them to look very carefully at the object to be drawn before they begin. Initially they should look at the object or animal through their 'window' or viewfinder, concentrating on the surface rather than the outside shape. They should then place the window on their paper and attach it with a small piece of sticky tape.

Using either pencil, coloured pencil, pastels or felt-tipped pens, ask the children to begin to do a very detailed careful study of the textured surface. Once they have filled the square they can move the window to another piece of paper and change their drawing material. Selecting the same or another section of the object or animal they are drawing they should then complete a second textured drawing. In total they should complete four drawings using a variety of media.

Follow by asking the children to do a much larger drawing on grey paper, working in the same style but this time using chalk and charcoal. Encourage them to start in the middle of the paper and work towards the edges thus avoiding the need to draw the shape until the interior has been completed. The earlier small drawings should help them in this task.

When completed the drawings should be sprayed with fixative to stop smudging. This is a smelly task however, and is therefore best done when the class has left the room.

Suggestion(s) for extension

There are many ways of experimenting with creating textures when working within the small window frames. Children who wish to experiment further could try working with wax crayons and adding a thin colour wash over the top or cutting and tearing papers to create a collage of the texture.

Suggestion(s) for support

The children should be able to complete the first task with little support. However, when they begin the second task it will be necessary to check that they are working to a scale appropriate to the size of the paper. Children find it easier to draw small rather than large and will need encouragement to fill the space.

Assessment opportunities

Collect all the children's pieces of work at the end of the activity and look through them. Return to the children with comments where appropriate offering praise and suggestions as to how they might improve their drawings. Add to your own notes on the children's progress where there has been some significant development.

Opportunities for IT

Try this activity using an art package. (See 'Opportunities for IT' in Feeling and drawing, page 78/79.)

Looking at works of art

Whilst Georgia O'Keeffe's large flower paintings have little textural quality they will highlight to the children the spectacular effects that can be achieved by working on a large scale. Her work can be found in many books on modern art, in particular in books on modern American art.

Display ideas

Displays which ask questions encourage the children to be involved. Make a display of the children's drawings alongside some of the objects that have been drawn. Put up a sign asking them to match the picture with the right object.

FIELDS AND HEDGEROWS

To explore the importance of texture and pattern in the art process.

†† *Whole class or small group. Small group for printing.*

🕐 *Three 45- to 60-minute sessions.*

Previous skills/knowledge needed

This activity requires some manipulative skills, including an ability to be able to cut, stick and organise a range of materials. It is best suited for children who are able to undertake these tasks with some proficiency.

Key background information

Children are required to produce a pattern in this activity, in order to experiment with a range of textures. Whilst they may produce an interesting pattern without further instruction, it is best if the pattern has some specific purpose. In this instance the children are asked to consider the patterns made by looking down on fields. It is not expected that the finished art work will have a 'polished' sense of aerial photography but rather that it will help the class or group understand that artists often create quite abstract pictures when expressing their understanding of the environment. Do not place too great an emphasis therefore on the pictorial aspect of this activity but rather concentrate on the children's ability to create a range of interesting textures, and their ability to manipulate the materials.

If possible, organise the classroom so that materials and art equipment are labelled and easily available to the children. They should be taught to get equipment for themselves and to clear away, replacing items at the end of the session. Where space makes this difficult, lay out equipment before the session so that it will be accessible to the children during the session. The children should become increasingly independent as they progress through the key stage.

Preparation

Provide sufficient wools, string and cloths for the children to work with. Photocopy pages 134 and 135 ready for use.

Resources needed

Wools, string, corrugated card, hessian, embossed wallpapers, other coarse fabrics, PVA adhesive, scissors, water-based printing inks, rollers, printing tray and newspaper. A piece of stiff card for each child, approximately 20cm x 15cm, rough paper, pencils, sponges, sheets of white paper, press print.

What to do

Use the two photocopiables to introduce the activity. Page 134 gives a few examples of the types of materials the children should look to collect and use and requires the children to produce a themed picture. There are two quite

distinct ways of working: either the children may produce an interesting collage and then decide upon a title (many artists, particularly the Surrealists worked in this way), or the title may be chosen at the outset and materials collected with a specific purpose in mind. If returning to this activity the following year you may try alternating the starting point to see which produces the best results.

The second photocopiable, page 135, shows a line drawing of a farmer looking for a lost lamb and is a useful starting point to remind children how important texture can be. The objective should be to add texture as well as colour. By using this as a starting point the children can try some textures out on this drawing and then do their own picture to which they add the texture through printing, rubbing, mark making and sponging. The final work may also be a collage.

For the main activity, give the children a piece of rough paper on which they can practise creating an aerial view of fields and hedgerows. Ask them to do two or three designs taking no more than three minutes on each. They should then select the one which they feel has the most interesting pattern. This can be copied onto their piece of stiff card.

Allow them to select from the materials available. 'Fields' can then be filled with strips of wool or spirals of string, or torn patches of corrugated paper. Similarly the hedgerows can be delineated by cut or torn pieces of embossed wallpaper, or fabrics lightly creased and crumpled as they are stuck onto the card. As they work the children should make sure that all materials are stuck down carefully, not leaving pieces to curl up, which may then become detached during printing. They should pack the card with detail leaving few, if any, blank areas.

Once completed the children should use their card designs as a block from which to print. Roll one colour out on the tray, then they can then ink up their cards and print onto white paper. The first print is often of poor quality therefore they should produce at least two and ideally three prints before washing their card to remove the ink. Undertaking three prints also provides an opportunity to practise the skills involved in printing.

Suggestion(s) for extension
Some children could go on to produce their design on a small sheet of smooth polystyrene (Easiprint or Pressprint is ideal). They can press the outline of hedgerows and fields into the polystyrene using a pencil and explore to see how many different textures they can achieve in each area.

Suggestion(s) for support
Give support to those children who find the cutting and sticking difficult especially if they become concerned that they are losing their original design. All children will continue to need support with the printing process and this task is probably best undertaken with no more than two children printing at one time.

Assessment opportunities
At the end of the activity review the outcome with them. Ask some of the children to show their final prints, talking about which sections they feel were particularly successful and which they found difficult. Be prepared to offer comments yourself, identifying children who have worked carefully or produced a particularly interesting section or effect using a material not used by others. It is important to find time to evaluate their work with them from time to time so that completed work is not 'dismissed' without acknowledgement of their achievements.

Opportunities for IT
Extend this activity using an art package to draw different field designs, perhaps using a spray to give the idea of

hedgerows. They can then experiment with different effects and colour tones to try and create the idea of texture in their own pictures

Looking at works of art

A number of twentieth-century British artists, particularly those painting in the St Ives area, have produced paintings of the coastline which have abstract pattern qualities. Try to find some examples by Patrick Heron or Ben Nicholson to show the children, see the book references, page 67. Discuss the shapes, colours and patterns which the artists use.

Display ideas

Take one print from each child and put one work on each page to make a book of their prints. The children can then add a brief statement about their work. Each child may start 'My print reminds me of...'.

Reference to photocopiable sheets

The title, 'The scary desert' (photocopiable page 134) should be regarded as just one of many titles that might be chosen to make a textured picture. The second photocopiable, page 135, shows a line drawing of a farmer looking for a lost lamb and provides a useful starting point for reminding the children how important texture can be in giving a picture interest.

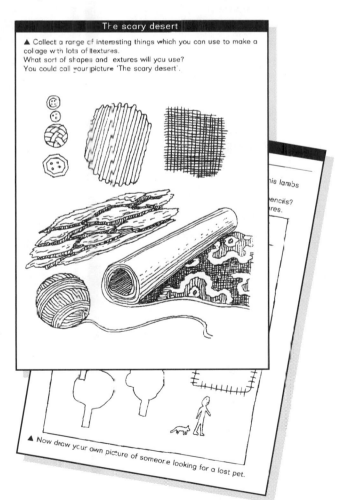

The scary desert

▲ Collect a range of interesting things which you can use to make a collage with lots of textures.
What sort of shapes and textures will you use?
You could call your picture 'The scary desert'.

▲ Now draw your own picture of someone looking for a lost pet.

JOURNEY TO THE CENTRE OF THE EARTH

To explore the basic qualities of weaving using a variety of materials.
†† *Small group or whole class.*
🕐 *Two 45- to 60-minute sessions.*

Previous skills/knowledge needed

This activity introduces the children to weaving. The class or group should however have experienced making, selecting, organising and evaluating their work. It is most appropriate therefore for children in Year 2.

Key background information

Textiles is an important part of the art curriculum, although time will dictate that it can only be undertaken on a limited number of occasions. When preparing the art scheme of work it is important to ensure that the children regularly draw, paint and model or construct. Within each key stage however they should also be given access to textiles, printing and more formal design work. Through discussion with colleagues these opportunities need to be planned into the overall curriculum for the key stage.

Prepare looms in advance (see illustration page 88). To begin with you may try giving the children two or three different types of loom, some using simple card looms and others a small wooden frame. After this first attempt the children should be taught to prepare their own looms.

Preparation

Prepare the looms before the session, preferably with additional help. In order to provide a wide range of materials from which the children can select, ask the children to bring in items from home. Explain that they are going to make a weaving and that they should collect as many varied and interesting materials, wools, papers and materials as possible. Supplement their collections with materials you have been able to collect. If there is a very wide range of items or if the whole class is to undertake this task at the same time then split the children into groups of five or six so that they can pool and share the materials.

Resources needed

As wide a range of papers, fabrics and wools as possible (especially in strong vibrant colours), one loom per child.

What to do

Discuss with the children the idea of a journey to the centre of the earth. What do they know about what is beneath them? If they were to travel in a glass lift looking out, what colours would they see as they passed through soil, clay, stone, rock and finally to fire?

ART

Texture

Once the children's imaginations have been stirred supply the group, or groups, with the basic equipment, a loom each and an assortment of materials already provided.

Beginning with fiery reds encourage them to work through the 'earth' perhaps going from reds to browns to whites and yellows and then greens. Finally as they break out of the ground they can move to the blues of the sky. As they work, encourage them to use the widest possible range of materials but ensure that they push down hard and tuck in the ends so that their weaving remains intact. They should not worry if their lines do not remain straight, indeed this is likely to add to the design rather than detract.

Suggestion(s) for extension

Children who particularly enjoy the process of weaving should be given the opportunity to experiment further. It is the type of activity which, once set up, can be undertaken at break or lunch-times and needs very little supervision. Suggest that two or three children work together on a larger, more ambitious weaving in which they use an old bicycle wheel or section of wire netting as the loom. The starting point for the weaving can be varied: suggest they choose a season (Autumn), or an event (Carnival), and develop their weavings using an appropriate range of colours, textures and patterns.

Suggestion(s) for support

Give help to those children who have difficulty with the process. Whilst it is normally inappropriate to demonstrate directly on the child's work, there is nothing more demoralising than working at a process which is going wrong and for which you do not have the necessary skills to put it right. If the child's weaving begins to fall apart because the materials are not being woven tightly enough then be prepared to intervene and offer the necessary support.

Assessment opportunities

Observe how well the children work together in groups. Note those children that are not only confident in undertaking their own work but are also able to offer help to others. Add to your notes kept on the individual development of each child where further significant development is apparent. Often in art work the progress being made by children is more apparent during the activity than when looking at the outcome at the end of the session.

Looking at works of art

There are a number of books devoted to textiles which contain examples of the work of weavers who use a range of materials in their work. If available share some of the examples with the children so that they can begin to understand the versatility of the medium.

Display ideas

When displaying their final weavings place each one in front of a sheet of black paper so that the full impact can be seen. Where colour is such an important factor in the work, considerable impact may be lost if the work is displayed in front of a brightly coloured background.

88

ART

THE VICAR AND HIS SISTER

To explore the uses of a wide variety of textures to create a relief portrait. To raise awareness of the physical properties of ageing.

†† *Whole class or small group.*

🕐 *Three 45- to 60-minute sessions.*

Previous skills/knowledge needed

This activity is designed for older KS1 children. It requires them to respond sensitively to the stimulus and to use materials and colour in a specific way.

Key background information

Much of the art work the children undertake involves imaginative work or drawing directly from observation. If we do not make careful preparations it can become very process-dominated. In other words, we spend a great deal of time introducing the children to a wide range of techniques without allowing them sufficient opportunities to talk about and express issues which concern them. Art is one way in which young children can come to a better understanding of the world in which they live, and they must be given opportunities to express their opinions about issues which are important to them. Thus they should be given opportunities to draw pictures of their family, other close relations, their friends and pets.

This activity is based not only on exploring a new process but also on helping children to better understand the process of ageing. In this instance talking about the issue is of equal importance to the art work. In the act of talking they can be as engrossed at looking at the world as they are when making direct observations.

Preparation

Display the Peter Rush poster (from the separately available pack accompanying this book) in the classroom for two or three days before the session so that the children can look closely and discover things for themselves. When you introduce the activity you can then remove it and ask the children if they have looked at the poster and what they can tell you about it. In this way you can stimulate the children to look out for changes to the display in the classroom, never knowing when they might be asked to comment.

Prepare for the session by asking the children how much they have observed. Return the poster to your wall and ask them to have another look and to describe it in detail. Besides asking them about the artist's use of colour and texture, ask them also about the characters of the people. What do they think the Vicar and his Sister are thinking about as they sit there? How has the artist made them look old? How old do the children think they are? As old people sit quietly what are they considering: are they reflecting on all the good things of life or are they rather sad? Use this as an introduction

into asking them about older people that they know. What sort of things do they think that older people worry about or what is it that makes them happy and laugh? (Pages 152 and 153 provide background information about Peter Rush and further questions that you may wish to ask the children.)

Collect a wide range of papers, prepare the wallpaper paste and photocopy pages 150 to 153 before the session.

Resources needed

Poster of *The Vicar and his Sister* by Peter Rush (in the pack accompanying this book), a range of papers, wallpaper paste, paste brushes and scissors, a stiff piece of card each (approximately A4 size), paints, brushes, water pots, rags, mixing trays and newspaper. Copies of photocopiable pages 150 to 153, one copy each of pages 152 and 153; sufficient copies of page 150 and 151 to allow one per child. Photocopiable activities require: clay, hessian boards and rolling pins, balloons, papier mâché, old spectacles and hats.

What to do

Start the activity by introducing the children to the Peter Rush poster, as outlined in the 'Preparation' section. Talk about the physical process of growing old, exploring with them how the skin begins to harden and wrinkle, how lines begin to appear in the face and the hairline recedes. Use the poster as the starting point for these discussions and allow sufficient time for the children to make their own observations before introducing them to the main sculpture activity.

Consider using the photocopiable page 150 at this point. The accompanying text suggests that the children should complete a drawing; you may decide instead to ask them to make a small clay tableau. Working in groups of four the children could make clay figures to represent the Vicar and his Sister as well as his two grandchildren. By drawing the scene first the children will have completed an illustration that they can use as a starting point for their sculpture.

Explain that you require the children to make head and shoulders portraits of either the Vicar or his Sister using papier mâché. They will not need to make their figures exactly like the people in the poster but they should attempt to make them look very old. They should begin by building up the face in relief on a sheet of A4 card.

Texture

Newspaper can be used to build up the basic form and, except when building up the nose, the children should not need to scrunch up paper. This can be very messy and they will achieve better results by steadily building up the layers. This will take a little longer but explain that they are not trying to build the face up completely but simply to give their portraits some depth.

Once they have built up the basic profile they can add the texture of the skin, hair and clothes. Thus when they apply the skin they should push the paper around, creating creases, and may also use a textured paper rather than smooth. The hair can be produced by cutting and curling paper before applying it. Use buttons or plastic counters for the eyes and a range of textures for the clothes.

When they have completed the textured surface the children can then add paint. However, if at this stage the children have created some very interesting art work then it may not be appropriate to undertake the painting. Always be prepared to adapt the activity if circumstances dictate.

Finally, look at photocopiable page 151 and suggest the children model a head using blown-up balloons with layers of papier mâché. Once they have achieved this suggest they use various props to complete some actual characters.

In his work, Peter Rush uses a whole range of props including a bench, clothes, a cup and saucer and some binoculars. The photocopiable suggests two props that are easily collectable and will help bring the sculptures to life, but you may decide not to use the idea of glasses and hats but experiment with other props instead.

Suggestion(s) for extension

If the final work is not to be painted consider asking the children to do a portrait painting of the person they have just created. Discuss colour with them, asking them not to spend time trying to use blues, greens and reds to create a very expressive painting, rather that they should concentrate on attempting to create a true skin colour.

Suggestion(s) for support

Those children finding difficulty with the papier mâché work may need some support, particularly if they work slowly and fall behind. Make sure that they work with quite large torn pieces of paper to build up the surface as quickly as possible. Ensure also that they produce high quality craftsmanship; the portrait will not look at its best if pieces of paper are not properly stuck down.

Assessment opportunities

Discuss the finished portraits with the children. In this instance there is a specific intention, to make the people look as old as possible so you can evaluate with the children who has created the oldest person! What is it about the particular work chosen that makes the person look so old? Add to your notes identifying those children who have shown a particular aptitude for this method of working.

Looking at works of art

Other artists have created moving portraits of people in their old age. One or two of Rembrandt's late self portraits are particularly haunting and well worth discussing with the children. These are readily available in art books. There is also a wonderful drawing by Van Gogh called *Old man with his head in his hands* which graphically illustrates a man's despair and is a lovely example to show the children.

Display ideas

Ask the children to make frames for their portraits. They should use four strips of card which they can stick to the edge of their card picture. Add lengths of string and press down tin foil over the top to create an 'embossed' frame.

90

ART

References to photocopiable sheets

Photocopiable page 150 asks the children to speculate what may be happening 'off camera' and on page 151 an alternative to exploring the idea of old age is used, and considers the use of props in making the sculpture more interesting. Pages 152 (background information about the artist and the poster) and 153 (key questions to ask the children) provide further resources to support your work.

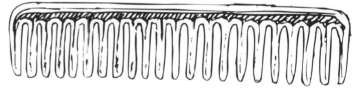

NEW LIFE TO OLD FABRICS

To use a wide range of textures to enhance pattern work.

†† *Small group or whole class.*

🕐 *Three 45- to 60-minute sessions.*

Previous skills/knowledge needed
The children will need to have had some experience of mixing colours to make others.

Key background information
The purpose of this task is for the children to explore texture through using a large variety of textures to create a pattern. By beginning with a flat pattern the task will be easier for them. It is also useful for the children to look at the work of designers, in this case a fabric designer, so that they can better understand how a professional creates two dimensional pattern from a three dimensional starting point. Whilst all the class or group could work from the same pattern it will add to the activity if the children are able to choose for themselves from a selection of fabrics.

Preparation
Collect a range of suitable fabrics with large floral patterns. An old pattern book would make an ideal starting point.

Resources needed
Various pieces of fabrics with large, simple, floral patterns, paper, paints, brushes, mixing trays, rags and newspaper. Various materials to create textures including combs, feathers, sand, adhesive, wax crayons and so on.

What to do
Ask the children to select one of the fabric materials available and then to choose the most interesting section to copy onto their sheet of paper. Ask them why they have selected their particular piece of fabric. Help with this task by supplying them with a 'window' cut out of a piece of paper which they can scan over the fabric in order to choose the section of the fabric they wish to draw. (The window should be approximately 20cm × 15cm.) Ensure that they create their copy of the pattern at least the same size as the original pattern, if not larger. If they make their shapes too small they will find it takes far too long to add the textures.

They should now prepare the textures they will use to fill in the shapes. Rather than copying the colours in the fabric, ask them to imagine they are creating a different coloured interpretation. They should work the flowers and leaves in

ART

tones and hues of one colour and the background in another. The background can then be in-filled using a flat colour wash.

Ask the group to experiment making a variety of textures on a number of small pieces of paper. They can add things to the paint, for example sand and adhesive, to make it textured or stick pieces of bark or fabric to the paper and then paint over them. As they build up the range they can begin tracing the shapes from their design onto the textured papers, cut them out and stick onto the design. Whilst they can work directly onto their designs this will not allow them sufficient opportunity to experiment or to make adjustments as the work develops.

It will be useful if the children share their textures as this will save time and resources. It will also encourage them to discuss progress and to share ideas.

Suggestion(s) for extension

Try the same task using coloured papers from magazines. The children should look for colours which are not 'flat' but have a texture, for example if they are working with green they should cut out hedgerows and trees which will give a mottled green. Rather than tracing and cutting out the shape they could add small strips to the area to be collaged, building up a mosaic.

Suggestion(s) for support

Ensure that the initial drawing is of the correct size and be prepared to intervene asking the child to redraw the design if it is too small. It is important that a good start is made to any project; there is nothing more disheartening than working for some considerable time on a project that is flawed from the very beginning.

Assessment opportunities

Make a point of highlighting to the class where children have produced good results through collaboration with the rest of the group. Where children have also produced interesting textures give them the opportunity to share the process with the rest of the class.

Looking at works of art

Children need to have the opportunity to explore the work of artists, craftspeople and designers and whilst we often refer to the work of artists, we tend to ignore the work of designers. This is a good opportunity therefore to look at the work of fabric designers and the activity of looking at the various fabric designs collected, comparing them, seeing how they repeat, and deciding which they prefer is equally as valid as looking at paintings.

Display ideas

Whilst their finished work will make an interesting wall display, consider putting the ideas together and making up a class pattern book.

Form

The study of form offers children the opportunity to construct, model and design three-dimensionally using a variety of materials. Through these activities they are introduced to space and form and they learn to manipulate shape spatially. We live in a three-dimensional world, which the children explore in early dance, drama and PE lessons. So too in art they need opportunities to explore three-dimensional space and shapes.

Many adults find it more difficult to express ideas and thoughts working three-dimensionally than with pencil or paint. Three-dimensional work is also more difficult to organise in the classroom and certainly more difficult to store. It is therefore generally given less prominence in the art curriculum than it requires. It is important however that children at all stages of their art education are given the opportunity to work three-dimensionally.

Working with recycled materials is a cheap option and allows children the chance to construct, join and manipulate materials in an expressive way. They are far less daunted than any adult would be at being asked to turn a few kitchen rolls, egg boxes and small cartons into a robot or the Houses of Parliament!

Junk materials alone are an insufficient diet however. Provide opportunities for the children to use other more traditional sculptural materials, for example salt dough, clay, wood, card and paper as well. Working with these materials requires the children to learn a range of basic technical skills including cutting, joining and gluing. They also need to learn something of the processes involved and to evaluate their own work as they go being prepared to make changes where necessary.

PAPER SHAPES TO PAPER FORMS

To explore the relationship between shape and form using simple paper cut outs.

†† *Small groups.*

🕐 *Three 30- to 45-minute sessions.*

Previous skills/knowledge needed

This is an introductory activity and as such requires no specific previous experience.

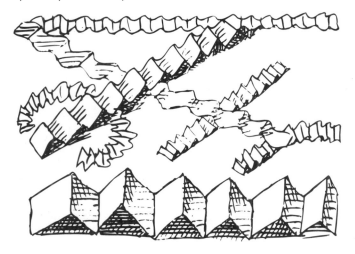

Key background information

Shape is inherent in almost all the activities in each chapter of this book. In addition, however, children require regular opportunities to move beyond shape to study form: three-dimensional shape. As soon as the shape begins to bend and come away from the paper then it becomes form. Young children are equally as happy to tackle form as they are all the other elements of art. If, however, they are not given sufficient opportunities to explore and make forms and use three-dimensional materials then their ability to work three-dimensionally remains underdeveloped. Generally teachers at KS1 do tend to make more opportunities to try three-dimensional work available than their colleagues at KS2, but three-dimensional work needs to be more than simply giving children the opportunity to do junk modelling.

As the children work, use questioning to prompt them to assess what they are doing. Ask: Do you think you need to fill that space? What sort of shape would look best with the ones you have already made? Can you think of a good way of joining those two shapes together? By doing this, the children will constantly be required to consider carefully the distribution of their shapes rather than sticking them on without sufficient consideration.

It should not be necessary to physically intervene in the children's work except to help with technical processes, for example, cutting an intricate shape which the children require but cannot do for themselves.

Preparation

Discuss the learning objective with any adults who are supporting you in this session, before you begin. Prepare some appropriate questions to ask as the children work (see Key background information above). Copy page 136 for the extension activity as appropriate.

Resources needed

A range of brightly coloured papers, scissors, adhesive and sheets of background paper (approximately A4 size). Photocopiable page 136 for the extension activity.

What to do

Give each child two sheets of brightly coloured paper and ask them to use one sheet to cut out a series of different sized strips, and to use the other as the background. The strips should then be folded, concertina style, both to make them stronger and to make them fold up and lift them off the surface of the paper. Before they stick their shapes down ask them to consider whether they want them in lines or criss-crossing. They may also try weaving them. Once they have decided, they can then stick the shapes firmly into place.

Continue by giving each child three different coloured papers and asking them to cut different types of shapes from each. For example, a child could cut square shapes from the blue paper, round shapes from the red and strips from the green. They can again explore cutting and folding to change the shapes before arranging them and sticking them onto a backing sheet.

ART

Try also producing sculptures rather than a relief. Give the children one piece of paper, approximately 20cm × 15cm, which they roll up and stick the two ends together to form a cylinder. They can then cut strips and circles from the other two colours to decorate their cylinders, adding shapes which tumble out of the top or from the two ends if the cylinder is laid on its side.

Suggestion(s) for extension

An alternative method of producing a three-dimensional form is to give the children small cardboard boxes and tubes to work with. Start by asking them to imagine what they would like to keep in their boxes.

Hand out the photocopiable page 136 and use it to inspire the children to work on their boxes. They may like to make a box for a chocolate egg in which case they should use bright red and smooth rounded shapes, or alternatively a packet of flower seeds which would encourage them to make large petal shapes. Start by covering the boxes in plain coloured paper and then let the children build on the folding exercise by making shapes and forms which fit their specific purpose. Having cut out different shaped pieces of paper and card they can then stick them on the boxes. Tearing the shapes can be as interesting as cutting and may prove easier for some of the class or group. More able children may even try joining their forms together by using strips of card.

Suggestion(s) for support

When creating their initial designs by sticking the shapes on paper, young children will tend to stick each item separately, without overlapping them. Be ready to ask them to try overlapping and weaving the shapes to produce more interesting patterns. Children with limited mobility may require support with cutting although they should be encouraged to do this for themselves even if the result produces some shapes with very ragged edges.

Assessment opportunities

Assess the children's initial abilities with cutting, gluing and designing. If this is their first three-dimensional work keep and date it or make a note of the outcome in your individual records on the children. If you are keeping the work as a record of their achievements and progress, make a brief note on the back of the work and mention if the child has been given some specific support.

Display ideas

There should be some very colourful outcomes to this activity. To display, either pack each set of reliefs and sculptures very closely together to form a mass of shapes, or take the work of a few children who have made a notable effort and display their work in sequence showing how they have moved from creating paper shapes to paper forms.

Reference to photocopiable sheet

In the main activity the children should experiment with a wide range of possible folds; start the photocopiable activity on photocopiable page 136 by asking the children what they wish to keep in their box.

ME AND MY HOUSE

To develop motor skills required to manipulate malleable materials. To be able to express personal views using a three-dimensional material.

†† Small groups.

🕐 Three 30- to 45-minute sessions.

Previous skills/knowledge needed

No specific skills are needed as this is an introductory activity giving children the opportunity to experiment and manipulate salt dough.

Key background information

Young children need regular opportunities to develop their motor skills. The best materials for supporting this development are dough, Plasticine and clay. Because dough is the softest and most malleable it is sensible to introduce them to this medium first. The stimulus for this activity is children and their own houses, however, a great many other starting points will produce equally valid and interesting outcomes. For example, you may ask the children to make fish, cakes or other foodstuffs which can then be used to 'stock' your play shop.

Preparation

You may decide to mix the salt dough before the session, however, the children will come to understand the process better if they observe the ingredients being mixed at the beginning of the session.

Making salt dough

Salt dough is made with: 2 measures of plain flour to 1 measure of salt; a dribble of cooking oil and water to mix.

Mix the ingredients and knead the dough into a workable consistency.

At the end of the session bake the finished work in an oven at 100°C for approximately 2–3 hours.

Once baked, the models can be painted and varnished. Use basic water-coloured paints or felt-tipped pens and a clear polyurethane gloss or satin varnish.

Resources needed

Small pieces of paper, pencils, dough, knives, clay modelling tools or wooden lollipop sticks, felt-tipped pens or paints and brushes, mixing trays, rags, polyurethane gloss or satin finish varnish and a clear polythene sheet. Access to an oven.

What to do

Start by talking to the children about the houses in which they live. Ascertain some facts such as whether they have an upstairs or a chimney, how many windows they have on the front of the house and so on. Ask them to make a drawing of the front of their houses on a small piece of paper which can then be retained to be the design sketch from which they will work when modelling the dough.

If you haven't yet mixed the dough, mix it now with the children having a turn at adding the ingredients, mixing and kneading. Explain the process to them as you mix. Explain also that while the dough is very soft at present when it is baked a chemical reaction occurs and the dough then becomes very tough.

Lay the polythene sheet over the table and give each child a small ball of dough. Allow them to experiment for a few minutes, pressing their fingers into it, rolling it into a sausage, squeezing and pinching. This allows them to get a feel of the properties of the dough and to better understand how they can use it when making their models. Provide as much time as the children need to acquaint themselves with the properties of the dough; although there is no specific outcome to this part of the activity it is nevertheless important and it is essential to give it sufficient time.

The children are now ready to make their house. Ask them to each flatten out a lump of dough to about ½cm thick, then referring back to their drawings cut out the basic house shape using a knife. Add windows, a door and a chimney and press into the dough with a clay modelling tool to create some texture. If you intend hanging up the houses, ask the children to press a paper-clip into the back of their models before they are cooked to make a clip for hanging. Once completed the models can be cooked.

In the next session the children can paint their houses, using a fine brush for the detail or felt-tipped pens if this is too difficult. Encourage them to mix bright, vibrant colours.

The group will now have a good understanding of the process and should be given the opportunity to consolidate their learning by making a self-portrait of themselves to

accompany their houses. They can use the same process, again experimenting with textures as they work. Rather than asking them to do a drawing first invite them to work directly with the dough. Give them a small extra piece on which they can practise textures before attempting them on their models. Before cooking, remember to add a paper-clip pressed into the back to enable the models to be hung up. Paint and varnish the completed work.

Suggestion(s) for extension

Children who show good control can try cutting out their windows on their houses, using a cocktail stick rather than sticking the windows on. Encourage them to add other details, for example making the house with the door open and adding window frames in the spaces.

Suggestion(s) for support

Throughout the process bring to the children's attention examples of good work, or interesting textures that others have produced so that the children become used to sharing their achievements and ideas. Demonstrate to the children where necessary but avoid doing the work for them.

Assessment opportunities

If this is the first time the children have used a malleable material then make brief notes on each child indicating their level of ability. As you observe a significant development or effort on the part of a child, add to the page of notes you are slowly building up on each child.

Display ideas

If you have inserted paper-clips into the back of the models, the work can be easily pinned or nailed to a board. Group the models close together to produce an effective pattern of houses and people.

PEBBLES, PINCHPOTS AND PEOPLE

To further develop manipulative skills and to understand some of the basic properties of clay.

†† *Small groups.*

🕐 *Two 45-minute sessions.*

Previous skills/knowledge needed

No particular skills are needed as this is an introduction to clay. It will be beneficial however if the children have undertaken some simple modelling using salt dough, such as the activity, Me and my house, on page 96.

Key background information

Whilst many of the children will already have had experience of working with clay, remind them of the rules for successful modelling (see page 82 for general advice on using clay). Clay is a versatile material and ideal for using with quite young children. Provide regular opportunities for the children to work with clay throughout Key Stage 1.

Preparation

Photocopy page 137 as required. As with some painting and drawing activities it is advisable to try out the activity yourself before the session, especially if you have little experience of working with clay. In particular try making a pinchpot.

Resources needed

Clay (earthenware clay is preferable to 'new' clay which has an unpleasant texture and is rather more difficult to manipulate), a small piece of hessian or a wooden board for each child to work on, clay modelling tools, clay knives and newspaper. Provide a small bowl of slip which will be useful although not compulsory at this stage. (Slip is very wet clay watered down to the consistency of sticky mud, used as glue to join pieces of clay together.) Photocopiable page 137 as required. Poster of Moore and Giacometti's work (from the separately available pack accompanying this book).

What to do

Prepare by covering the table with newspaper, giving each child a piece of hessian or a wooden board and making modelling tools and knives available. Give each child a lump of clay which will fit comfortably in the palm of one hand. Allow them plenty of time to pull, squeeze, pinch, slap, roll and poke the clay, exploring its possibilities.

Follow by asking the children to break their clay into four equally sized pieces and to make a series of basic shapes; suggest a cube, sphere, cone and pyramid. Can they make the sides really smooth and all the sides of equal size? Can they now join their shapes together to produce another interesting shape?

ART

The three pieces of clay can be rolled back together, slapping the clay firmly and rubbing the surface with their fingers to erase the creases at the joins. Ask them to now make a very smooth pebble, as smooth as any they might find on the sea shore. Once this is completed they can then roll the fourth shape they have retained into a long thin sausage and use this to decorate their pebble, pressing strips firmly to the surface creating wavy lines. Make the bowl of 'slip' available in case the children need some help in joining their pieces together.

Develop the activity by asking the children to make simple pinchpots. Whilst good results can be achieved by placing the ball of clay on the table, pushing your thumb into it and then pinching the clay to slowly turn the ball into a simple pot, it will be much better if the ball of clay is held in the left hand and turned round as the right hand is used to gently pinch the edges. Remember that the best results are often achieved by coaxing and squeezing the clay rather than by treating it roughly. Remember too that when in contact with the children's hands the clay will quite quickly begin to dry out and so it should be handled sparingly. It is possible to sponge the clay lightly with water but this is difficult for young children and it will be best to work with the clay without recourse to sponging. The children should work quite slowly and carefully, in order to get the clay as smooth and thin as possible without the edge cracking.

Complete this first activity with clay by asking the children to make a person from a lump of clay, carefully 'pulling out' the legs, arms and head. If possible, they should avoid sticking pieces on, completing the person from the original piece of clay. Ask them to make the person stand and once the main shape is completed suggest that they use a modelling tool to add details.

Finish by using the photocopiable page as an inspiration for some crazy clay creatures. The children now have the opportunity to create forms without worrying about the size of legs or arms, or achieving the correct shaped head. As they work, ask them if they feel they are making interesting shapes. Is their figure fierce, brave, frightened? At this age the children's imaginative drawings and sculptures can be delightful. Encourage them all to be proud of their individual achievements.

Suggestion(s) for extension

Once the children have mastered the technique of pulling the clay they can make a number of small figures, sitting, kneeling or lying down. At this stage encourage them to make interesting smooth forms rather than trying to create 'fiddly' additions to their models.

Suggestion(s) for support

With clay work it may be necessary to directly support the children when they are making their models or pots, in order to help them solve problems. For example, helping them to make a figure stand when the legs have been rolled too thin.

Assessment opportunities

Observe the children closely whilst they are working, taking note of those children who show a special aptitude for clay work or those who find clay a more difficult medium to use than paint or pencil. You will discover that a number of children will be better able to express themselves three-dimensionally than through drawing. Again add to individual notes on the children where appropriate.

Looking at works of art

Look at the Henry Moore sculpture on the Moore and Giacometti poster in the separately available pack accompanying this book. It is highly likely that Moore started this model on a small scale working with clay. Discuss the sculpture with the children and compare it to their figures. Do they think they could make one in the same style?

Also show the children the work of artists such as Miró, Klee, Picasso and Henri Rousseau to reinforce the idea that there are many ways of representing the human form.

Form

Display ideas

Rather than saving all their initial clay work ask the children which of their pieces they like best and retain only these. (Recycle the remainder by putting the clay into a bin and adding sufficient water to cover it. Leave until the clay has absorbed the water then place the clay onto a wooden board and knead until sufficiently pliable to be re-used.)

Display their chosen pieces on cloth or paper covered boxes rather than on a plain, flat surface. The children might like to design and paint a suitable background themselves to display behind their models.

Crazy land

Welcome to Crazy Land!
Its strange creatures are half human, half animal.

▲ Use clay to make some creatures to put in your own Crazy Land.
▲ Add lots of interesting textures to make them really crazy!

Reference to photocopiable sheet

Whilst it is important that children are given opportunities to draw and model people, slowly developing the ability to produce increasingly realistic interpretations, it is also necessary to give them sufficient opportunities to develop their imaginative work. The idea therefore of producing creatures for an imaginary land (photocopiable page 137) allows children to experiment and to use their imaginations with some clay modelling.

PATTERNS IN STRUCTURES

To develop understanding of three-dimensional pattern through using and organising three-dimensional objects.

†† *Small groups.*

🕐 *Up to four 45-minute sessions.*

Previous skills/knowledge needed

This is an introductory activity and therefore requires no previous experience. The children will, however, be required to join and stick materials as the activity develops, and some manipulative skills will therefore be required.

Key background information

This activity introduces children to making structures using plastic cups, plates and egg cartons. It also encourages them to explore making structures that are based on repeated patterns. It is important that the children have regular opportunities to undertake three-dimensional work as a good number of children (and adults) will be able to express themselves more confidently working in this way rather than through drawing.

Preparation

Brief any adult helpers before the session. Ensure that the necessary materials are readily available for the group to use. Photocopy page 138 ready for the extension activity.

Resources needed

Building blocks, construction kits, drinking straws, sticky tape, string, egg cartons, plastic cups, plates, paints, brushes, scissors, stapler, drawing paper and pencils. Copies of photocopiable page 138 as necessary.

What to do

Begin the activity by letting the children use the building blocks and construction kits which you have available. Ask the children to use the building blocks to make a patterned structure in which they try to repeat simple arrangements. If they find this difficult ask them to look at the way bricks are arranged in a built wall and suggest that they copy this. Ask them to think of another way to 'bond' the blocks to create a structure. How many different ways can they use the blocks to build a wall?

ART

Working with the construction kits the children can make 'boxes' which they then add onto or stack up, working in all directions. Ask them if their patterns are more interesting if they are all the same size and shape, or when they are varied.

Further sessions

Develop the work which the children have done with construction kits by introducing them to making their own structures using drinking straws. Before beginning to assemble the straws, the children may like to decorate them by painting them or if using plastic straws the children can stick small strips of coloured paper around them.

Ask them to make a whole series of triangles using the straws. Join the straws initially by using Plasticine, sticky tape or adhesive. When they are dry the children can tie the joints with string, coloured wools or ribbons. This will add to their designs and patterns. The children should now consider the various ways in which their triangles can be joined together to make an interesting structure.

Further structures can be built by joining paper plates or cups together, either sticking or taping together, or cutting a simple slit into them so that they can be slotted together. Ask the children to draw circles using the cup or plate as a template, paint them and then cut out and stick them down symmetrically or asymmetrically to make a pattern.

Similar results can also be achieved by using egg cartons. Prior to joining or stacking the cartons suggest that the children try to paint or decorate the inside sections, aiming to repeat colours or shapes to produce an interesting and imaginative pattern.

Suggestion(s) for extension

Use the photocopiable page with children who successfully used the individual items. It is often helpful to set restrictions rather than allowing them free access to the 'junk modelling' box and children find it equally challenging to work within constraints as when given a very wide brief; indeed they often respond more positively when they are clear as to what is and is not permissible. With this activity they are asked to work with three boxes, three lids, three paper cups and six straws that provides a quite specific challenge. The combinations for models are endless and a wide range of outcomes should result. If the children want to add colour to their machines, restrict the choice to perhaps three colours.

Suggestion(s) for support

Provide practical support wherever necessary during these tasks. The children may need assistance with holding the straw triangles whilst they are assembling them.

Assessment opportunities

Talk to the children at the end of the activity in order to assess how much of the process they have understood. Can they describe what they have done and how their pattern works? How could they improve the final structure? If they have worked as a team what part did they play? Although there is not always sufficient time, it is important to evaluate the activity and the children's understanding of the process. This can be ascertained from discussions with them, or during 'show and tell' sessions at the end of the lesson.

Display ideas

A useful resource for any school is a series of simple chipboard display stands which can be stored flat and then quickly assembled when required. Cover these display stands with white cloth and arrange the children's structures adding labels indicating the objective of the task. If spheres have been made, these are best displayed by hanging on a thread from the ceiling or from a beam.

Looking at works of art

A number of modern sculptors use multiples of one particular shape in the production of their work. Look in the library for books on twentieth-century sculpture.

Reference to photocopiable sheet

The accompanying photocopiable activity (page 138) can be used as an extension to the main activity, once the children have experimented with making designs from repeating shapes. The page prescribes a precise number of items and challenges the children to make a machine from these items.

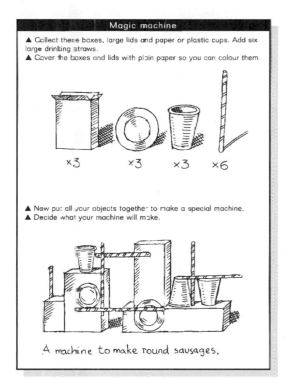

Magic machine

▲ Collect these boxes, large lids and paper or plastic cups. Add six large drinking straws.
▲ Cover the boxes and lids with plain paper so you can colour them.

×3   ×3   ×3   ×6

▲ Now put all your objects together to make a special machine.
▲ Decide what your machine will make.

A machine to make round sausages.

DANCERS IN THE AIR

To record observations accurately and quickly. To develop collaborative ways of working and sharing ideas. To develop pattern making and three-dimensional skills.

†† *Whole class.*

⏱ *Three 45- to 60-minute sessions.*

Previous skills/knowledge needed

This activity is best suited to children in Year 1 or 2, who have already demonstrated an ability to record their observations with reasonable accuracy.

Key background information

Giving the children differing amounts of time to undertake a drawing helps them to realise that the length of time taken on a drawing is not necessarily proportionate to the quality of the outcome. Children of all ages enjoy the challenge of working very quickly on short, sharp tasks with constant reminders to hurry up. The children should use their drawings as designs from which to make mobiles, working in pairs. It will not be necessary for them to worry about detail. For the purposes of this activity an outline of the figure will suffice.

Preparation

Ensure that the children will be able to see the figure posing when undertaking the initial drawing exercise. This may require some reorganisation of the classroom or arrangements made for the children to work in the hall and producing their drawings while sitting on the floor. Make a copy of photocopiable page 139 for each child.

Resources needed

Six pieces of drawing paper (A4 or slightly smaller) per child, sheets of coloured card approximately 15cm × 10cm sufficient for three sheets per child, cotton thread, sticks of approximately 30cm length, coloured papers, scissors, soft drawing pencils, adhesive, coloured papers, tin foil, paint or crayon. Copies of photocopiable page 139 as required.

What to do

Tell the children that they are each going to produce six figure drawings in the first session. Each drawing must be completed in five minutes, and they must fill the whole of the piece of paper. Explain they should not worry about detail or background but concentrate only on the outside shape. Thus they will each create a series of six silhouettes.

Try a timed practice drawing so that they can see how fast they will have to work and how difficult it is to make the drawing fill the paper. Be 'strict' and make them stick to the rules. Tell them not to worry overly about the proportion of their figures but to try to capture the essence of the pose.

Ask one of the children to take up the first pose – standing in a star shape – and ask the children to do their first drawing. The model will need to rest his or her arms at times but should still be able to retain the pose for the prescribed length of time.

At the end of the five minutes allow the children to 'rest', look at their drawings and prepare themselves for the next drawing. Discuss how the next drawing could be improved. With each pose ensure that the model takes up an interesting position, for example with one leg on a chair as if in the act of stepping or with arms raised as if reaching up.

By the end of the session the children will have produced six drawings that should highlight considerable improvements between first and last.

The children should continue the activity working in pairs, with each child copying three of their drawings onto coloured card making any adjustments they consider necessary. The figures should again fill the space. The children should then cut out their drawings and add some decorative design.

At this point it would be very beneficial to look at one of Matisse's late cut out figures. This would show the children how striking designs can be made without being over-fussy. If a copy of Matisse's work is not available then equally interesting results can be achieved by asking the children to cut out two or three quite simple shapes and sticking them onto both sides of their silhouette. Ask the children to use complementary colours; for example using reds to green or purples to yellow to get a very striking effect. Working in pairs they should discuss how to make their figures reasonably similar to each other's.

Once the figures are completed the pairs of children can punch holes in the figures, add cotton thread and tie them to the sticks. They will need to work very closely together to get their mobiles to balance and may require some assistance from you.

Extend the mobile work by using photocopiable page 139. The children are required to use mathematical shapes to make mobiles and they will discover that by drawing two repeating shapes, cutting slots and joining them together they can make simple three-dimensional shapes.

The designs will look much more interesting if the children decorate their shapes before they put them together. This will set them a further challenge; some may be able to decorate their shapes so that when they are joined together the patterns link. The best results will be obtained by sticking on brightly coloured papers and tin foil, although paint or crayon can also be used.

Suggestion(s) for extension

The children could use their original drawings to make cut outs. Unroll a large sheet of black paper across the floor and tape it down. Ask the children to select their two best drawings, cut them out and lay them onto the black paper. Two or three children can then arrange the cut outs to produce an interesting pattern.

Suggestion(s) for support

Some children will find the drawing task especially hard. Urge them not to give up. After each drawing ask them to compare it with their previous attempt rather than with other members of the class so that they can judge for themselves how quickly they have improved. Remind them that it is the shape and pattern that are important not the proportions.

Where there are difficulties be prepared to help those pairs who cannot balance their mobiles.

Assessment opportunities

This activity offers the opportunity for a range of assessments to be undertaken. Consider the children's attitudes to the quite demanding drawing task, their ability to work in pairs and the quality of the craftsmanship of the finished mobile.

Opportunities for IT

The children could use an art or drawing package to make copies of their three best hand-drawn pictures, focusing on the shape and pattern rather than proportions. If their pictures do not fill the screen the children can alter or re-size the shape. They may need to alter the orientation of their paper from landscape to portrait before they begin drawing. Limit the children to a few brush or pencil sizes. Once the shapes have been drawn the children can use the fill options to colour them in contrasting or complimentary colours. The final figures can be printed, cut out and mounted on card.

An alternative approach would be to print out the figures onto an ink-jet OHP acetate sheet. The printed figures could then be cut out so that they made a transparent mobile. You may need to add some weighting to get the light acetate to hang properly.

Looking at works of art

There are two artists, whose work may make a significant improvement to the quality of this activity. Alexander Calder produced a whole series of brightly coloured mobiles. Showing one or two of these to the class would help the children to understand how intricate the balance of a mobile can be and how pure colours placed next to each other can enhance the quality of shapes. Observation of Henri Matisse's simple collages will also help the children understand better how shapes within shapes can produce wonderful balance and harmony. Both artists' work is quite accessible, in books on twentieth-century art or in books specifically devoted to the individual artists.

Display ideas

Hang the children's mobiles from a string stretched across the classroom, or from strings pinned directly into the ceiling.

Reference to photocopiable sheet

Mobiles provide a good source for three-dimensional work. In the main activity, however, the children are working essentially two-dimensionally until they put their mobiles together. Photocopiable page 139 encourages the children to investigate mathematical shapes to make some interesting mobiles.

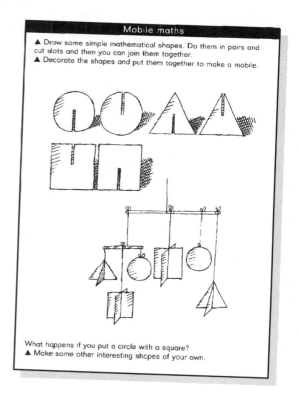

Mobile maths

▲ Draw some simple mathematical shapes. Do them in pairs and cut slots and then you can join them together.
▲ Decorate the shapes and put them together to make a mobile.

What happens if you put a circle with a square?
▲ Make some other interesting shapes of your own.

INTRODUCING MASKS

To improvise with a range of materials to create masks.
To use the masks to create role-play situations.

✝✝ *Small groups working in pairs.*
🕐 *Three 45- to 60-minute sessions.*

Previous skills/knowledge needed

This activity is designed for children who have demonstrated the ability to work confidently with a range of materials. Ideally this should be undertaken with children in Year 2, towards the end of Key Stage 1.

Key background information

The relationship between art and literature provides a wealth of starting points for art work. In particular drama offers considerable scope for children to engage in creative art work. Designs for scenery, costumes and posters provide children with opportunities to undertake art work for a specific purpose using a wide range of skills. There is however a very considerable difference between asking children to design and make (for example, a mask) and the teacher deciding on the play, the costumes and masks, limiting the child's role to filling in, or decorating adult drawings and constructions. In these instances the child is unlikely to be covering the requirements of the National Curriculum, and at best, learns a very specific craft skill only.

When linking art and literature through a proposed drama production be very clear as to the learning objectives before including the activity in the art programme.

Masks also have great significance in many cultures and you may wish to use this activity as a way of introducing another culture. The accompanying photocopiable is loosely based on Maori masks and further examples are not difficult to find in art or travel books.

Preparation

Collect the bases for the masks before the session, checking they are of an appropriate size. Ensure there is a sufficient range of materials in the 'scrap bin' for the children to have a good choice when decorating their masks. You may decide to ask the children to bring in some suitable fabrics and papers from home, if so, make your request in advance of the planned sessions. Make sufficient copies of photocopiable page 140 to allow one copy per group.

Resources needed

Provide at least three types of base for the masks, each with a very different shape (large paper plate, cardboard box and strong paper bag), scissors, adhesive, pencils and paints, paintbrushes, a range of materials from the 'scrap bin' (include shiny papers, fabrics, tin foil, tissue and activity paper), newspaper and wallpaper paste for papier mâché work. Copy of photocopiable page 140 for each pair or group.

What to do

Introduce the activity to the children by discussing with them the idea of staging their own play. Tell them that it should include as many characters as there are in the group, but suggest that there are two of each type of character and the children can work in pairs making two similar but not identical masks. There is no need at this stage to decide the details of the plot.

Ask the children: Who are the children to have in their play? Will there be people, monsters or animals? Are the characters going to be angry, sad, kind or ugly? Will they be old or young? Once these decisions have been made they should choose the base which they feel will best suit their character. For example, they may consider a kind person would have a round face and so they may choose a paper plate as the base. Alternatively the character may be very

angry in which case they may decide upon the cardboard box. By providing at least three differing bases they will, from the outset, be working towards creating very different types of characters.

Holding the base to their faces, they can decide upon the location of eye and mouth holes with their partners. They may be able to cut these out themselves or may require the help of an adult. Working together the children can decide upon the method of decoration.

Try and involve the children at an early stage by asking them to bring in scraps from home. Collecting resources and materials is an important element in children's artistic development and should be built into the activity. However, make sure that there are also sufficient resources available to support them.

Allow the children considerable freedom to choose how they decorate their masks. Show them how to begin by building up the surface to shape the nose, eyebrows or any other prominent feature. This is an important stage, for if the children build up the surface using papier mâché the finished results will look far more interesting. They may also require some technical help, for example sticking on a nose made from a paper cup, or cutting the corner off a cardboard box to make it less angular. In this, the traditional roles are reversed with the child producing the design and the adult providing the support! When the children come to decorating their masks there is no reason why they should not be left to work unaided.

Once the masks have been completed the children can then begin to work on their play in drama lessons.

The accompanying photocopiable, page 140, provides an alternative mask-making idea to the main activity. Whilst it is more restrictive in that it requires a specific mood and style to be adopted it nevertheless provides a wealth of possibilities. Try to find some other examples of Maori masks for the children to look at before they begin. If some children have made 'fierce' masks in the original activity compare them with these masks and consider what they have in common. Again ask them to discuss and consider an appropriate range of colours to use before beginning the decoration process.

Suggestion(s) for extension

The children may decide they require costumes to accompany their masks, as well as other props or some very simple scenery to use in their play and can be encouraged to develop these themselves.

Suggestion(s) for support

The emphasis in this activity is on the children making decisions and choices for themselves. The need for some technical help has already been considered, however, the children will also need to be questioned and prompted with ideas which will in turn make them constantly reconsider the

options open to them. 'What would the effect of putting...' or 'Have you considered...' will make the children continually review progress as they work.

Assessment opportunities

Use the activity to look for evidence of the children's ability to make decisions for themselves or in conjunction with their partner. Look also for evidence of the child's creative ability, in particular their ability to collect and use materials in a creative way. Add to your individual notes on the child, noting progress in these areas.

Looking at works of art

Whether or not you decide to base this activity around masks from other cultures it is very helpful to provide a range of masks from around the world for the children to consider.

Display ideas

One of the purposes of display is to inspire others; this is particularly true of art displays. Once the plays have been acted out and the masks displayed, retain two or three of the most interesting for exhibiting before you next try this activity. Children will often better understand the requirements or potential of an activity if they can see how other children have tackled it and this in turn will inspire them to improve on what they have seen. Asking the children if you can retain examples of their work for showing to others should therefore be a regular part of many of the activities.

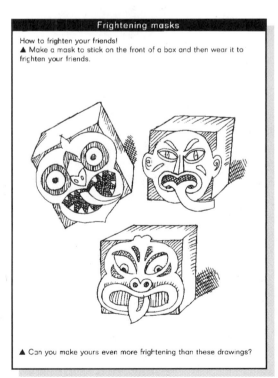

Frightening masks

How to frighten your friends!
▲ Make a mask to stick on the front of a box and then wear it to frighten your friends.

▲ Can you make yours even more frightening than these drawings?

Reference to photocopiable sheet

Photocopiable page 140 provides a stimulus for the children to design and make a Maori style mask.

SKINNY PEOPLE

To identify the characteristics in the work of a famous artist and to use the understanding and knowledge of the artist's work to inform future art work.

†† *Small groups.*

🕐 *Three 30- to 45-minute sessions.*

Previous skills/knowledge needed

This activity requires some technical competence and is best suited to Year 2 children.

Key background information

Whilst we often want to tap in to children's imaginations and allow them the freedom to interpret subject matter in their own way, increasingly art educators have re-emphasised the value of children looking at the work of famous artists and using their observations to work in a similar style. This is equally as important in the development of children's three-dimensional skills as it is in aiding their progress in painting and drawing. There are difficulties: the children cannot feel the texture nor walk around the sculpture if their observations are from books and there are also often difficulties in the technical aspects to be overcome (in this instance the Giacometti is a bronze sculpture). Nevertheless with some careful planning these problems can often be overcome.

Preparation

Spend a little time looking at the poster of the sculptures, based on the theme of 'The Body' by Moore and Giacometti in the separately available poster pack accompanying this book, before the session. There are a number of questions on photocopiable page 157 which will give you ideas for the discussion although you will probably want to ask other questions as well. In particular you will need to discuss the feelings that the Giacometti inspires and to ask the children whether they can think of ways they could produce a

sculpture in the same style. Page 156 provides some background information about the poster. Photocopy pages 154 to 157 as required.

Resources needed

Poster of 'My Body' showing works by Henry Moore and Alberto Giacometti (in the separately available poster pack accompanying this book). For photocopiable page 154: clay, base boards, sponges (slightly dampened to smooth the clay), forks, sieves, rough pieces of bark to create coarse textures. For the main activity: each pair of children will need three pieces of wood (one piece approximately 2.5cm square and 25cm in length and two others each approximately 10cm in length), cardboard, adhesive, bark, rough cloth, sand and very small stones, lump of clay per model, paints and brushes to finish. For photocopiable page 155: pencils, clay, boards and modelling tools. Extension activity: thin wire, Plasticine. Sufficient copies of pages154 to 157 as required.

What to do

Show the children the poster and discuss the contents with them, comparing and contrasting the two sculptures. After a little while focus their attention on the work by Giacometti. Be prepared to spend some time looking and discovering with the children and answering any questions they may have.

Whilst the poster introduces the children to twentieth-century figurative sculpture it is not necessary for all the work which follows to be essentially figurative. The notion of working with various textures is also important and the children may therefore undertake this work beginning with simple thumb pots. Use photocopiable page 154 to explore the idea of using rough and smooth textures, before beginning the main activity. Provide the necessary modelling tools and equipment so that the children can experiment with a wide range of textures.

Once they have explored this option, ask the children how they might make a sculpture of a body which looks as though it has been dug up after thousands of years! Even if you have already decided upon the materials and processes you wish to introduce it is still valuable to ask the children to offer their own suggestions as this helps them to understand the value of brainstorming for ideas. Ask them to see if they can produce a sculpture very similar to Giacometti's from the materials you have prepared.

Working in pairs, give each pair of children three pieces of wood. The first should be approximately 2.5cm square and 25cm in length and can be used for the body and head, while the other two pieces, approximately 10cm in length become the arms.

The children should then join the arms to the body, adding a small piece of cardboard between the two pieces of wood and another piece of card to build up the head. (See illustration on the next page.) These sculptures can then be left to dry ready for the next session.

Form

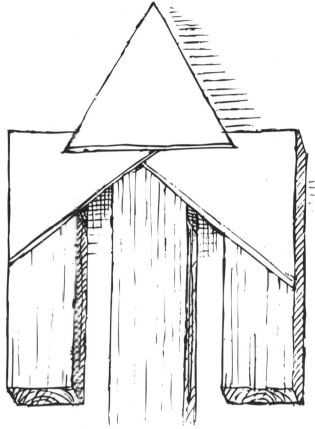

At the next session the pairs of children can add texture to the wood by gluing on pieces of bark, rough cloth and adding sand and very small stones. Try working on the texture with the figure laying down as this will be easier than working on an upright model. Once the figure has been thoroughly coated then the base of the sculpture can be pushed into a lump of clay which will both represent the feet and also provide a firm base for the sculpture.

The sculptures can either be left at this stage or painted in one colour to unify the various textures. When the children paint their sculptures it is advisable to add a little adhesive to the paint to ensure it adheres firmly to the surface.

Use photocopiable page 155 to finish the work and ask the children to draw their ideas of how the offspring of the unusual models on the poster would look. Encourage them to use lines appropriate to the style of the models. The task can easily be transferred into a three-dimensional activity by asking the children to use clay to make head and shoulder representations of the strange children they have drawn.

Suggestion(s) for extension

The children's figures may look as wooden as Giacometti's, as though the figure has never moved. Now ask the children therefore to experiment with various shapes of a figure in motion. Give the children several pieces of thin wire a ready cut to length, and a lump of Plasticine. Ask them to bend the wire to represent arms, legs and torso and to use the Plasticine to join the wire together. The children very quickly learn to experiment with a range of shapes and positions as they manipulate the wire.

Suggestion(s) for support

Give support to the children in any areas where they are having technical difficulties, for example when sticking the arms to the body. When the children are adding texture they will need to be reminded to break the bark into small pieces and to use small pieces of cloth. Point out to them that if they work with large pieces, the sculpture will quickly come to look messy and lose its form.

Assessment opportunities

Art activity provides children with the opportunity to suggest ideas, test out hypotheses, select materials and make adjustments and alterations. As the children work in pairs or as members of a small group take the opportunity to observe them working with others. When an adult, other than the teacher, is providing the support then it is important for the teacher to get feedback on how individual children have managed. For example, to check on how much support they have required, whether they fully understood the task and whether they were able to make a useful contribution to the discussion. Asking such questions not only provides useful information on the progress being made by the child but also helps the adult providing support to focus on the learning as well as giving technical support.

Looking at works of art

There are many books on Giacometti and his work features in books on modern art which include sculpture as well as painting and drawing. Show the children other examples of his work and they will quickly realise that long, tall, motionless figures are a 'trademark' of his work.

Display ideas

Try displaying the sculptures on a bench against a wall. Cover both the background and the top of the bench in white paper. You may even add two boards at right angles at the end of the section in which the sculptures are to be displayed to create a small 'gallery'. Place the sculptures within this space, allowing sufficient space between each so that the texture can be fully appreciated. This will help to give their work characteristics akin to that produced by Giacometti.

Form

Reference to photocopiable sheets

Photocopiable page 154 provides a modelling activity in which the children reproduce rough and smooth textures. (The next activity Coiling clay pots introduces the children to coiled pots and you may therefore decide to delay this photocopiable activity until they have tried this alternative method of pot making.) Page 155 develops the idea of rough and smooth but requires the children to draw rather than make. Pages 156 and 157 provide background information about the poster and some sample questions to ask the children to consider.

COILING CLAY PLOTS

To be able to use clay in a functional way to make a pot. To develop manipulative skills and to increase awareness of form and pattern.

†† *Small groups.*

🕐 *Three 45-minute sessions.*

Previous skills/knowledge needed

Whilst coiling looks easy, it is in fact quite a difficult skill and takes some considerable time, even for an adult, to become proficient. Quite young children can, however, produce good results using this process as long as they receive support where required. The children should therefore have had some previous experience of working with clay before attempting this activity.

Key background information

There are times when the boundaries between technology and art as described in the National Curriculum become blurred, particularly when the art activity has a functional outcome. You may therefore decide to talk to the children about producing a vessel which contains water or which you could drink from, discussing the properties it would need. These are primarily technological considerations. Artistic considerations will however be centred upon the form (or the aesthetics) of the pot, and with producing a sympathetic pattern for the surface. Whichever focus, either technology or art, both subjects require the children to learn to use materials skilfully. The development of good craft skills is therefore central to this activity.

Preparation

It is beneficial if you try this activity yourself before asking the children to attempt it. Start with quite a small lump of clay which you squeeze into a thick fairly cylindrical sausage. Lay it on a board or piece of hessian, and working from the centre of the clay use one hand and firmly 'seesaw' back and forwards working outwards to the edge of the clay. This will cause the clay to roll backwards and forwards becoming gradually thinner. Spend some time rolling coils until you can produce them to the approximate thickness of a wax crayon and at least 20cm long. Check that the consistency of the clay is neither too soft nor too hard.

The children will not complete this activity in one session and their work will need to be stored between sessions. To avoid the clay drying out, firmly cover their work with a polythene bag to stop the air getting to it. If the room is particularly warm you may also need to put a damp paper towel over the pot before covering with polythene.

Make a photocopy of page 141 for each group. Photocopiable page 154 may also be copied, if required.

Resources needed
Clay, craft knives, modelling tools, various items for creating textures on the clay (fork, comb, bark, sieve), hessian or clay board, 'slip' for joining, boot polish, varnish and wax crayons for reference, apples or similar shaped objects. Copies of photocopiable pages 141 and 154.

What to do
Give each child a fairly large ball of clay. Ask them to pull off a lump and to squeeze it into a sausage. Demonstrate to them how to roll out a coil using the method described above. Point out to them the importance of learning just how hard to press. Ask them to try themselves; provide wax crayons for the children to use as a template for gauging the correct thickness. Remind the children that if they make the coils too thin then their pot will need many coils and will probably collapse before it is finished.

When they have each rolled out five or six coils then they can begin to make their pots. Ask them to take their first coil, roll it round into a ring and join the two ends together. The best method for joining is to overlap the ends using a craft knife, cut through both ends at an angle and smooth together using their fingers or a modelling tool.

A second coil can then be added, laying it on top of the first and making the join at a different point. The children can either lay the coil exactly on top of the first or slightly towards the outside so that their pot begins to splay out. Be careful, however, not to come out too much with each coil.

When the children have produced a pot three or four coils high, ask them to add a base. This can be done in one of two ways. Either they can roll up a coil into a tight spiral, smooth out the creases and place their pots on top, adding slip first in order to achieve a good join, or they can roll out a piece of clay and follow the same procedure. Cut off any surplus clay using a craft knife.

Do not let the children be too ambitious with their first attempts; if the pots grow to 10cm this will represent a fine achievement. Discuss with them the pattern they might like to add. They may experiment first on a surplus piece of clay before starting on their pot. Ask them to keep their pattern abstract, experimenting with a range of textures rather than with attempting to draw specific shapes such as flowers or animals. Their patterns should ideally be in 'sympathy' with their pots: wavy, combed lines flowing around the form following the natural contours for instance. Finally they may either smooth the top of their pot or make indentations to create a wavy edge.

If it is possible to arrange to have their pots fired this will enhance the activity and make their pots more durable. They can then be boot polished if it is not possible to glaze them. Rubbing polish into the texture and polishing up it will help the texture to stand out more clearly. It is possible to paint the unglazed clay and then to add varnish, but if doing this make sure the colour does not detract from the emphasis on form and texture.

Young children will have found coiling quite demanding. However, once they have mastered the basic technique the activity will have more relevance if they can make their pots for a specific purpose. Develop this by using photocopiable page 141. Provide a small apple for each child and let them work through the 'apple pot' idea. Ensure that they keep measuring as they work, so that they do not allow their pots to grow out of control! The work will look even more interesting if, at the conclusion, they add some detail to the outside of their pots and make a lid. If undertaking this activity it is necessary to remember that the dry pot will have shrunk by at least 10%.

Suggestion(s) for extension

Let a group of children work together to create one large pot. Individually rolling out two or three long coils they can take turns in adding their coils under the direction of one or two children who can act as supervisors, deciding the overall shape required. The whole group can then be involved in deciding on the pattern, first drawing their ideas on paper, then discussing the options together and jointly deciding which pattern to use.

Suggestion(s) for support

Where children find difficulty rolling out the clay and become frustrated by their lack of achievement, be prepared to offer help, if necessary rolling out some coils for them. Stop the group at times and point out both problems others are having or examples where progress is very good.

Assessment opportunities

Whilst you will have noted the problems that the children encountered with the process, there will also be a finished product which it is possible to assess. Look at each of the children's pots, comparing their ability to create interesting forms, demonstrate 'high quality' craftsmanship and to produce patterns in keeping with the form. Make very brief notes on each child under these headings to add to your previous notes from other art activities.

Looking at works of art

Most manufactured pots are made from pouring clay 'slip' into a mould. If they are 'craftsman'-made then the likelihood is that they have been 'thrown' on a wheel. You may have some difficulty therefore finding a pot which has been produced by coiling the clay. Nevertheless, even manufactured pots allow you the opportunity to discuss with the children the wide variety of shapes and patterns used. In particular look for examples of textured pots rather than those with floral designs.

Display ideas

Cover a table with a white cloth and add a few small plants to the children's pots. Plants can significantly enhance exhibitions of the children's work. Lay some books flat under the cloth to raise some areas so that not all the pots are displayed at the same height.

Reference to photocopiable sheets.

Use photocopiable page 141 to provide a specific purpose for a coiled pot. Page 154 introduces another type of pot making and can be used in conjunction with this activity.

Photocopiables

The pages in this section can be photocopied for use in the classroom or school which has purchased this book, and do not need to be declared in any return in respect of any photocopying licence.

They comprise a varied selection of both pupil and teacher resources, including pupil worksheets, resource material and record sheets to be completed by the teacher or children. Most of the photocopiable pages are related to individual activities in the book; the name of the activity is indicated at the top of the sheet, together with a page reference indicating where the lesson plan for that activity can be found.

Individual pages are discussed in detail within each lesson plan, accompanied by ideas for adaptation where appropriate – of course, each sheet can be adapted to suit your own needs and those of your class. Sheets can also be coloured, laminated, mounted onto card, enlarged and so on where appropriate.

Pupil worksheets and record sheets have spaces provided for children's names and for noting the date on which each sheet was used. This means that, if so required, they can be included easily within any pupil assessment portfolio.

Making it move, see page 18

Birds flying

Name _____   **Date** _____

Here are three strange birds flying across the sky.
▲ Add some more interesting birds of your own, flying, swooping and gliding.
▲ Try and fill the whole area with all sorts and types of strange birds.

ART

Making it move, see page 18 and Using line imaginatively, see page 34

Stormy sea

Name _____   **Date** _____

Here is the start of a picture of a very stormy sea.
▲ Can you finish it by adding lots of swirling angry lines?
You could add a little boat in your picture being tossed about by the huge waves.

ART

Exploring moods, see page 21

Dangerous skies

Name _____   **Date** _____

This lady is standing on the edge of a field. She is very frightened.
What sort of horrible shapes do you think she has seen in the sky?
▲ Finish the picture. Try to make your picture look very threatening.

ART

Fruits, vegetables and plants, see page 24

Vegetable maze

Name _____   Date _____

Do you know what sort of vegetable this is? It looks like a maze.
▲ Use a pencil and go for a walk around the spaces.
▲ Try drawing a very complicated maze using lots of wiggly lines.

▲ Choose some other fruit and vegetables to draw very carefully using lots and lots of interesting lines.

ART

Lines around the school, see page 29

Through the door

Name _____   Date _____

Here is a drawing looking through two open doors in a house.
Can you count how many rectangles there are?

▲ Look around your classroom and see how many rectangles there
are and then try to draw them all.
▲ Leave out all the shapes that are *not* rectangles.

Drawing people, see page 31

Mother and baby

What sort of lines have been used to draw this picture?
Do you think they are suitable for this subject?

▲ Try drawing a picture of a mum who is cross with her child.
What sort of lines would you use in your picture?
If you add colour, what colours are you going to choose?

Mixing colours, see page 38

Colour mix chart

Name _____ **Date** _____

Mix the colours together to make this chart.

	White	Yellow	Red	Blue	Black
White					
Yellow					
Red					
Blue					
Black					

Now mix red, yellow and blue together in differing quantities.
How many different shades can you make?

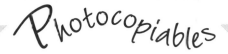

Fruit and flowers, see page 42

Fruit on a cloth

This patterned bowl and mat make an interesting background for some oranges and apples.

▲ Can you arrange some fruit on a piece of cloth or in a bowl so that you can draw and colour a picture like this? You may find it easier to set it up on the floor.

Stormy seas, sunny skies, see page 44

Street light shining

Name _____   **Date** _____

It is a cold afternoon. It is pouring with rain and the wind is blowing madly. The rain is bouncing off the pavement. All you can see as you hurry home is the street light shining out.

▲ Paint a picture to show the clouds, the rain and the wind. Try to use lots of cold, dark colours and put the paint onto the paper so that you can see your brushstrokes.

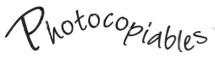

A colour sketchbook, see page 47

Through my window

Name _____   **Date** _____

Here is a sketch quickly drawn from a bedroom window.
▲ Mix lots of different greens to paint the fields.
What sort of sky can you see?
▲ Try mixing and blending together lots of different blues to make a really interesting sky.

Painting doors, see page 52

Boats on the sea

Here is a pattern drawn from simple but interesting shapes of boats. The boats are red and orange but the sea is green and blue.
▲ Draw a picture like this and paint it mixing lots of colours.

The box of many colours, see page 54

Under the sea

Here are some weird and wonderful shapes from under the sea.
▲ Copy some of them and add some more of your own. Then cut them out and stick them onto a box.
▲ Arrange some of them so they bend over the edge of the box.

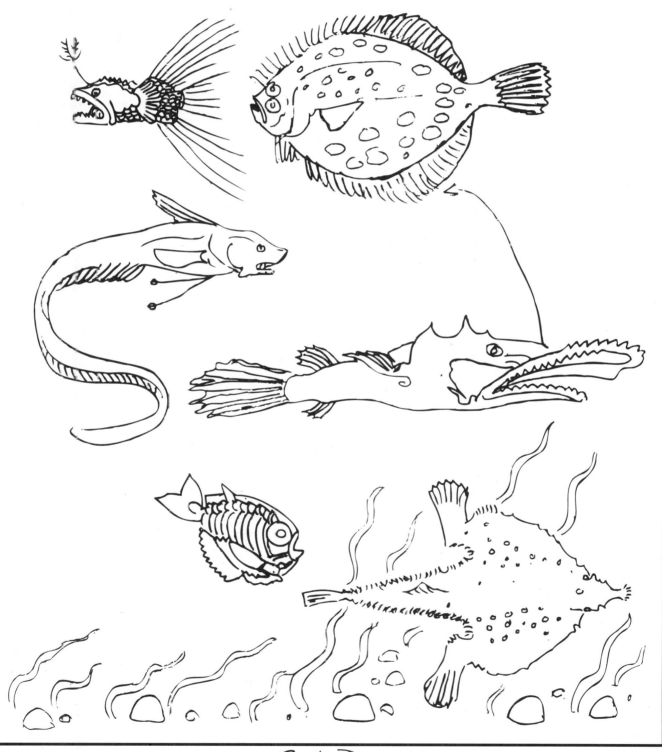

ART

Pattern through printing, see page 58

Walking line

Name _____   **Date** _____

Here is a line that wishes to go for a walk across the paper.
▲ Can you take it for a walk using a sharp pencil?

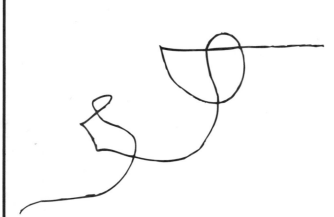

▲ Once you have finished 'walking' your line, colour in the shapes
you have made to make an interesting pattern.

Looking for patterns, see page 60 and Pattern through shapes, see page 67

Perfect pattern

What shapes have been used to make this pattern?
▲ Make your own pattern using only squares, triangles and circles.

▲ Colour this picture but try to use no more than four colours.

Curriculum Bank
125

ART

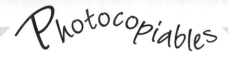

Patterns in buildings, see page 62

Building houses

Name _____ Date _____

Here are two houses all on their own. Imagine that the builders arrive and soon start building houses all around them. How many different types of houses might they build?

▲ Try to fill the paper, building houses next door and then along the road until you have completely filled the page.

Pattern through shapes, see page 67

Beautiful woman

Name _____ **Date** _____

This strange woman in her beautiful dress needs some colour.
▲ Paint her dress for her using bright and exotic colours.
▲ Add some background – she needs to be put in a very grand house against a brightly coloured wall.

Pattern in people, see page 72

People patterns

Name _____ **Date** _____

How would you describe this man? What colours would you choose to paint him?

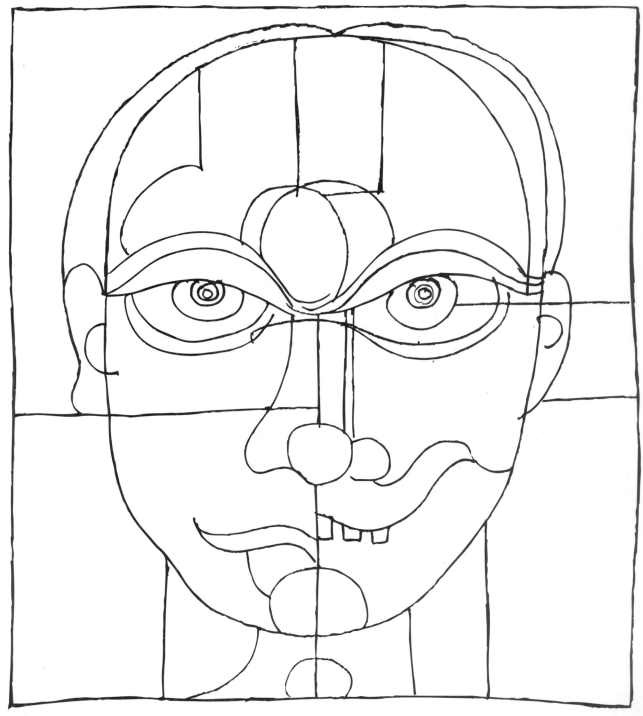

▲ Do a picture of your friend just using lines to make interesting patterns. Can you make your drawing as scary as this?

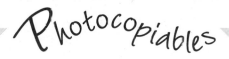
Mirrored pattern

Name _____   **Date** _____

▲ Complete this pattern by mirror-writing on the other half of the paper. If that is too difficult can you make a mirror pattern by writing your own name and then adding colour?

PATTERN

PATTERN

Feeling and drawing, see page 78

Touching textures

Which words best describe each of these textures?
▲ Can you draw some textures which are fluffy, rough, smooth, or prickly? Think of some other textures to draw as well.

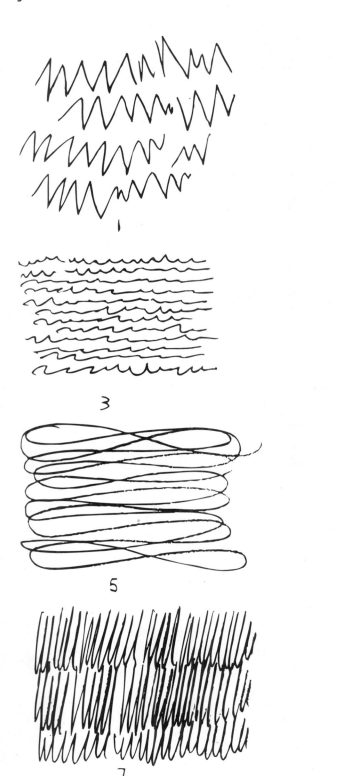

1

2

3

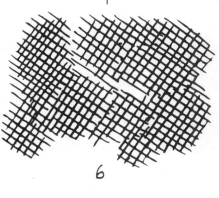

4

5

6

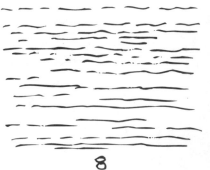

7

8

Rubbings and prints, see page 80

Make a rubbing

This is a rubbing from an old wooden beam. Can you imagine a pirate ship being rushed along in a violent storm when you look at this print?
▲ Do some rubbings of other textures and then make them into pictures of fields, skies or swirling seas.

Rubbings and prints, see page 80 and Pattern through printing, see page 58

Tracks in the snow

Footprints, animal prints and vehicles make an interesting picture in the snow.

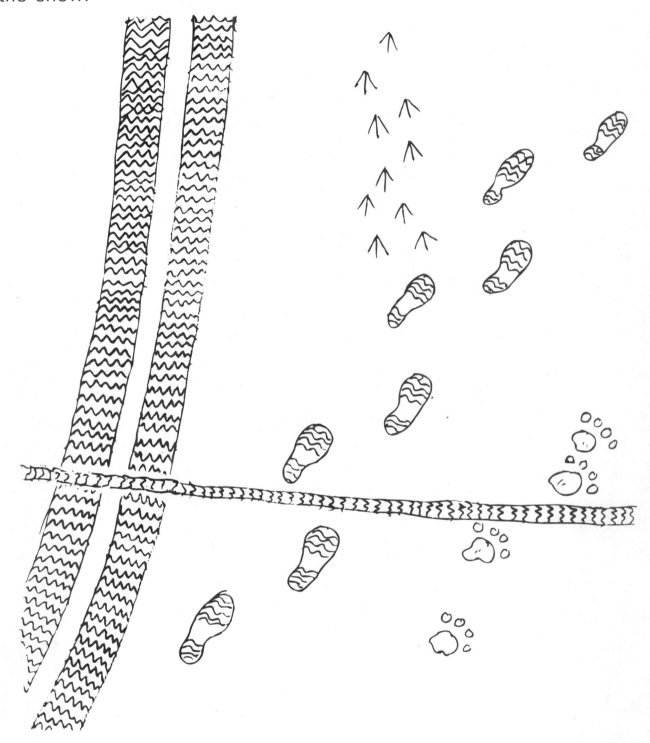

▲ Collect some toy cars, very small shoes and other items to make some prints. Now make an interesting picture from your prints.
▲ Practise printing on scrap paper first.

A magic garden

Here is a design for a paper doily.

▲ Collect some old pieces of lace or paper doilies and cut them up.
▲ Arrange them on paper to make a picture of a magical garden.

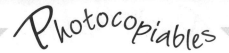

A close-up on trees, see page 82, Fields and hedgerows, see page 85

The scary desert

▲ Collect a range of interesting things which you can use to make a collage with lots of textures.

What sort of shapes and textures will you use?

You could call your picture 'The scary desert'.

Fields and hedgerows, see page 85

Lost lamb

Name _____   **Date** _____

This drawing of a farmer with his dog looking for one of his lambs was drawn by a six-year-old boy.

▲ Can you colour it in for him using pastels or coloured pencils?

▲ Use different sorts of shading to make interesting textures.

▲ Now draw your own picture of someone looking for a lost pet.

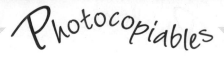
Paper shapes to paper forms, see page 94

The box of many shapes

▲ Make different shapes from strips of coloured paper.
▲ Use them to decorate a box. What would you put in your box?

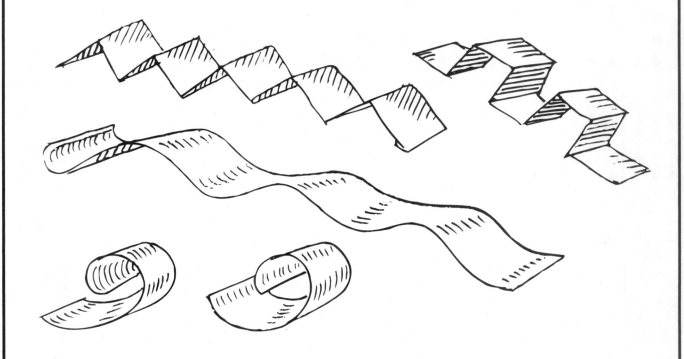

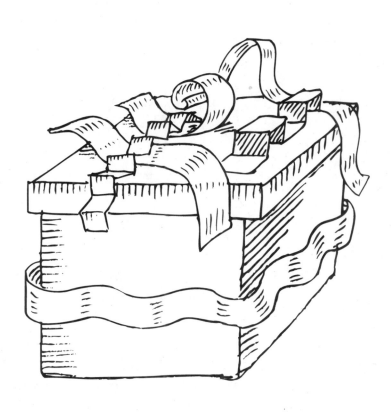

Pebbles, pinchpots and people, see page 97

Crazy land

Welcome to Crazy Land!
Its strange creatures are half human, half animal.

▲ Use clay to make some creatures to put in your own Crazy Land.
▲ Add lots of interesting textures to make them really crazy!

Patterns in structures, see page 99

Magic machine

▲ Collect these boxes, large lids and paper or plastic cups. Add six large drinking straws.
▲ Cover the boxes and lids with plain paper so you can colour them.

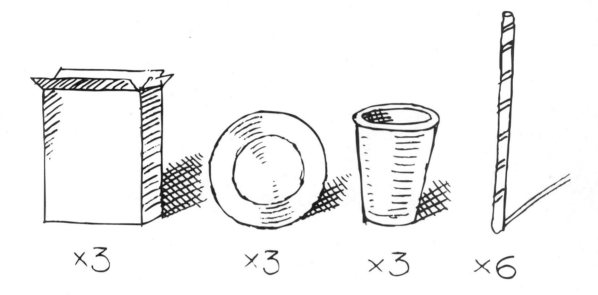

x3   x3   x3   x6

▲ Now put all your objects together to make a special machine.
▲ Decide what your machine will make.

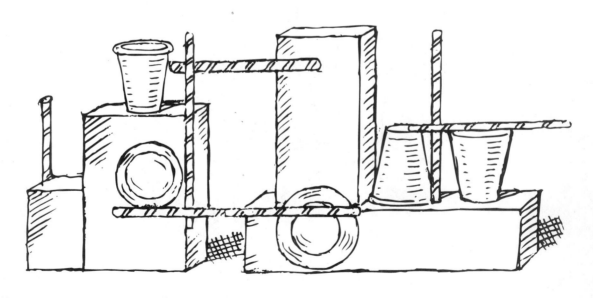

A machine to make round sausages.

Dancers in the air, see page 101

Mobile maths

▲ Draw some simple mathematical shapes. Do them in pairs and cut slots and then you can join them together.

▲ Decorate the shapes and put them together to make a mobile.

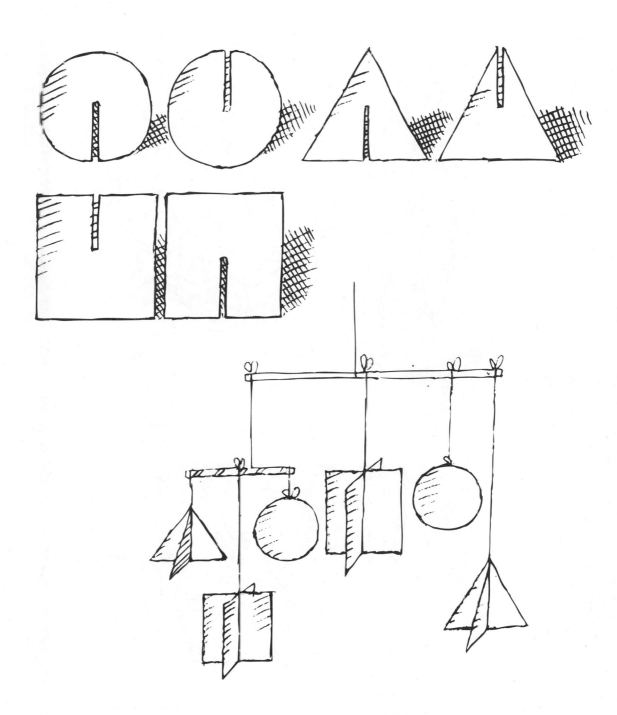

What happens if you put a circle with a square?

▲ Make some other interesting shapes of your own.

Introducing masks, see page 104

Frightening masks

How to frighten your friends!
▲ Make a mask to stick on the front of a box and then wear it to frighten your friends.

▲ Can you make yours even more frightening than these drawings?

Coiling clay pots, see page 108

The apple pot

Choose a good sized apple

Put your apple onto the piece of clay and cut round it with a knife to get the right size.

Make sure you smooth each coil in carefully using your finger, to get a good join.

Can you make a lid to fit?

How will you decorate the outside of the pot?

Drawing people, see page 31

Thanks Mum

Mums are always fussing, doing your hair, tying your tie and brushing your jacket aren't they?

▲ Can you do a picture of a mum looking after her son or daughter?
▲ Do some practise sketches first.

Drawing people, see page 31

Dad and children

The first go at riding my bike (with dad).

Artists often paint pictures of mums and their babies or their children, but it is very difficult to find a picture of a dad with a baby. ▲ Can you draw a picture of a dad with his baby or with his children? What sort of things do dads do with their children?

Drawing people, see page 31

Mary Cassatt

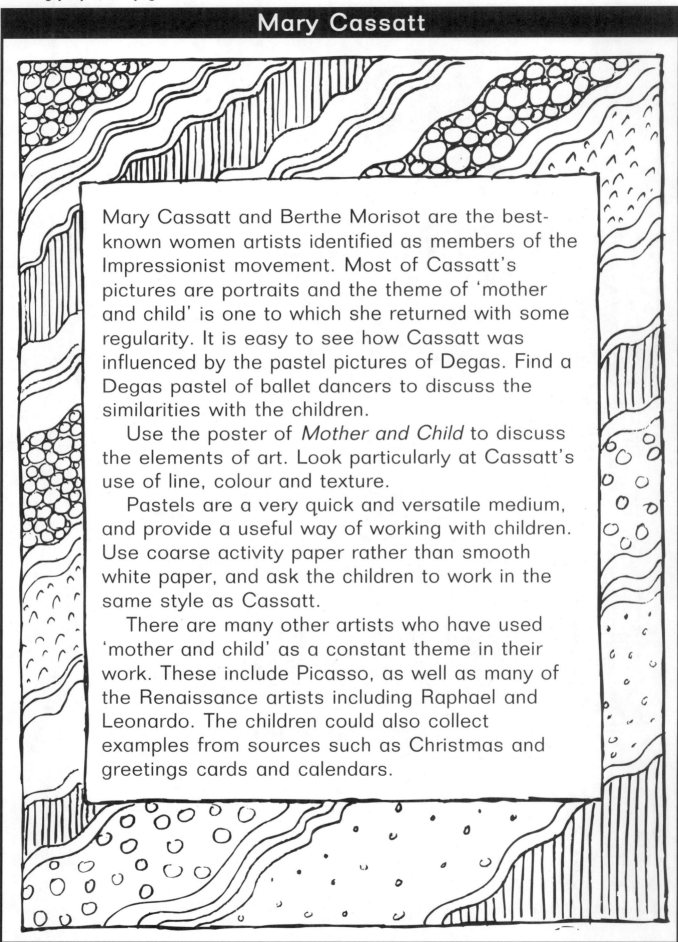

Mary Cassatt and Berthe Morisot are the best-known women artists identified as members of the Impressionist movement. Most of Cassatt's pictures are portraits and the theme of 'mother and child' is one to which she returned with some regularity. It is easy to see how Cassatt was influenced by the pastel pictures of Degas. Find a Degas pastel of ballet dancers to discuss the similarities with the children.

Use the poster of *Mother and Child* to discuss the elements of art. Look particularly at Cassatt's use of line, colour and texture.

Pastels are a very quick and versatile medium, and provide a useful way of working with children. Use coarse activity paper rather than smooth white paper, and ask the children to work in the same style as Cassatt.

There are many other artists who have used 'mother and child' as a constant theme in their work. These include Picasso, as well as many of the Renaissance artists including Raphael and Leonardo. The children could also collect examples from sources such as Christmas and greetings cards and calendars.

ART

Drawing people, see page 31

Mother and child key questions

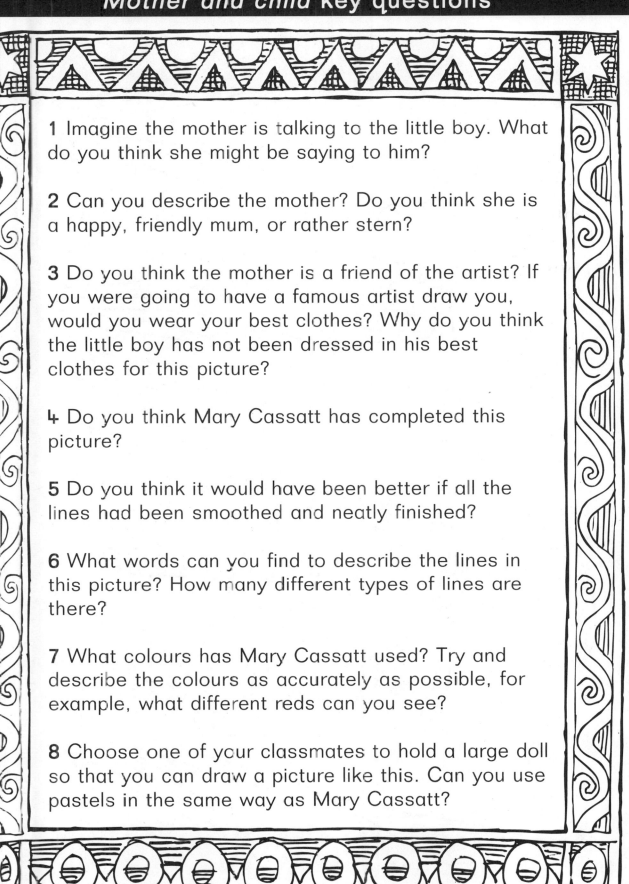

1 Imagine the mother is talking to the little boy. What do you think she might be saying to him?

2 Can you describe the mother? Do you think she is a happy, friendly mum, or rather stern?

3 Do you think the mother is a friend of the artist? If you were going to have a famous artist draw you, would you wear your best clothes? Why do you think the little boy has not been dressed in his best clothes for this picture?

4 Do you think Mary Cassatt has completed this picture?

5 Do you think it would have been better if all the lines had been smoothed and neatly finished?

6 What words can you find to describe the lines in this picture? How many different types of lines are there?

7 What colours has Mary Cassatt used? Try and describe the colours as accurately as possible, for example, what different reds can you see?

8 Choose one of your classmates to hold a large doll so that you can draw a picture like this. Can you use pastels in the same way as Mary Cassatt?

Van Gogh and colour, see page 49

Daffodils coming into bloom

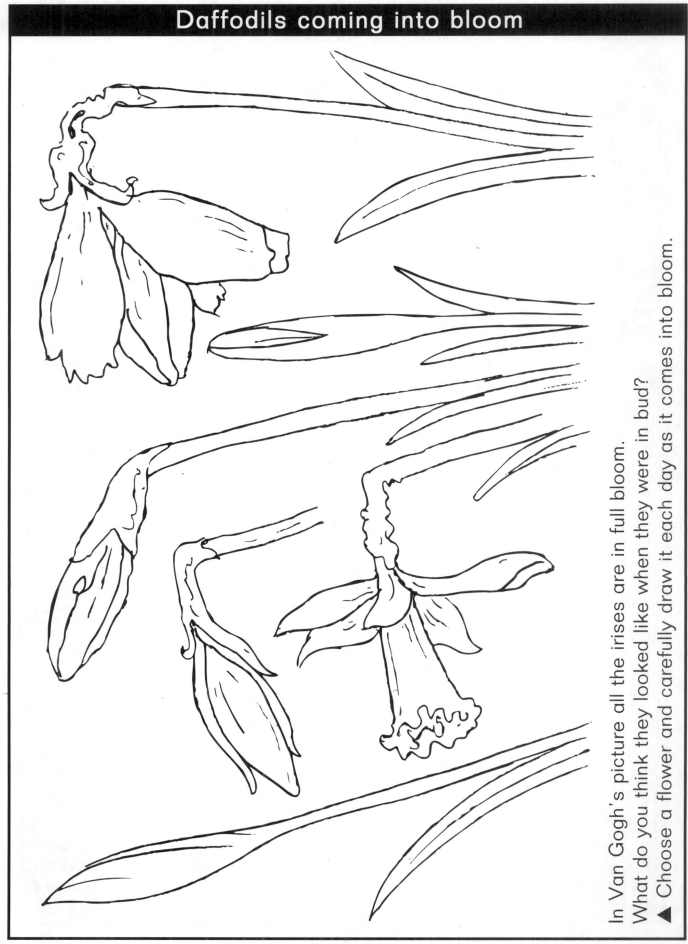

In Van Gogh's picture all the irises are in full bloom.
What do you think they looked like when they were in bud?
▲ Choose a flower and carefully draw it each day as it comes into bloom.

Van Gogh and colour, see page 49

Painting an iris

Which iris from Van Gogh's painting is this drawing a copy of?
▲ Choose just one of the irises and do a huge picture like this.
When you paint you will need to mix lots of different shades of blue.

Van Gogh and colour, see page 49

Van Gogh

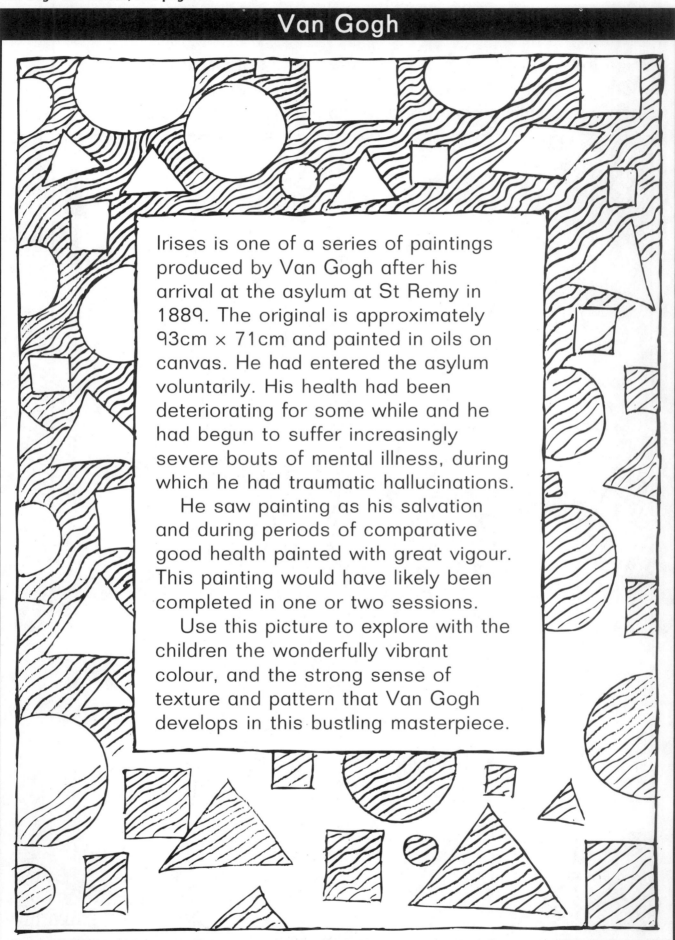

Irises is one of a series of paintings produced by Van Gogh after his arrival at the asylum at St Remy in 1889. The original is approximately 93cm × 71cm and painted in oils on canvas. He had entered the asylum voluntarily. His health had been deteriorating for some while and he had begun to suffer increasingly severe bouts of mental illness, during which he had traumatic hallucinations.

He saw painting as his salvation and during periods of comparative good health painted with great vigour. This painting would have likely been completed in one or two sessions.

Use this picture to explore with the children the wonderfully vibrant colour, and the strong sense of texture and pattern that Van Gogh develops in this bustling masterpiece.

Van Gogh and colour, see page 49

Irises – key questions

1 Look at the colour of the ground (earth). Can you give a name to all the different colours you can see?

2 Where do you think Van Gogh positioned himself to paint this picture?

3 Imagine touching the leaves, the flowers and the earth. Can you describe how they would feel?

4 Look carefully at the brushstrokes. How can you tell whether Van Gogh has put the paint on very thickly or thinly as if doing a colour wash?

5 There are lots of different types of lines. Look very carefully, can you describe some of them?

6 Just suppose we could visit this garden and sit where Van Gogh sat. Close your eyes and imagine. What smells would you notice and what sounds would you hear?

7 Now you have looked at this picture of irises, can you describe a 'real' iris flower? Imagine you are writing about this flower in a science lesson, what would you write?

8 Can you draw a picture of just one small area of your garden, or some flowers in the school grounds? Make sure your flowers stretch from the top of your paper to the bottom.

ART

The Vicar and his Sister, see page 89

The vicar's grandchildren

Name _____ **Date** _____

Here is a picture of the Vicar and his Sister's feet!
The space is left for a picture of the vicar's two grandchildren having a picnic on a rug laid on the grass.

▲ Can you draw and colour the picture? Do the vicar's grandchildren look like him? Ask your friends to pose for you.

The Vicar and his Sister, see page 89

Hats and glasses people

▲ Use a balloon and put papier mâché over it. When you have built up a few layers you can start to decorate. Can you make (or find) some spectacles to put on your people? Look out for an old hat too. This will help make your people look really interesting.

The Vicar and his Sister, see page 89

Peter Rush

Peter Rush lives and works in Dorset. He creates not only exquisite caricatures of the famous and more ordinary people through the medium of papier mâché, but is also a professional illustrator. His illustration work includes many years of drawing stories for Jackanory and illustrating the Heggerty Peggerty series of books.

Peter is a keen observer of human life. Use the poster to explore the character of the two people. Discuss with the children the facial expressions, postures and clothes as well as the activity portrayed.

Peter regularly works as an artist in residence with children of all ages. Working on a simple base frame he gets children to use paper towelling and kitchen rolls rather than newsprint. Dipped in wallpaper paste and modelled into position the results are often almost as interesting as his own work!

ART

The Vicar and his Sister, see page 89

Peter Rush – key questions

1 What do you think he is saying to his sister?

2 What words most describe the skin and facial expressions?

3 Why do you think the artist has made their skin look so white?

4 Why do you think his sister has binoculars round her neck? Where do you think the Vicar and his Sister are?

5 Do you think the artist can pick up the Vicar and his Sister and put them in chairs in a lounge? What sort of room do you think would suit them? What sort of things do old people have in their homes?

6 What sort of people do you think they are? How would you describe their characters?

7 Can you imagine them getting up from the chair and walking away? Can you act out the scene?

8 Can you draw a picture of two old people sitting on a beach in their deck-chairs?

Skinny people, see page 106

Rough and smooth thumb pots

Look at the texture on the two sculptures on the poster. Can you see how smooth one is compared to the other?

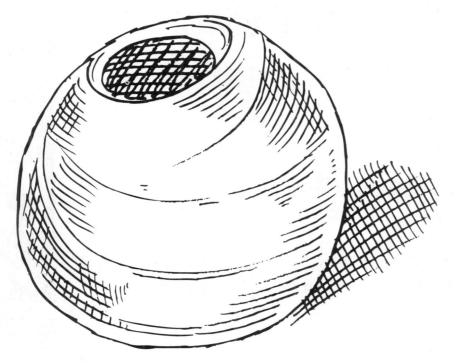

▲ Try and make two thumb pots like these and make the textures on each very different.

ART

Skinny people, see page 106

Mary Moore and George Giacometti

Name _____   **Date** _____

Imagine the two odd people on the poster have children.
▲ Draw pictures of these children, using lots of long flowing lines
for one and short jagged lines for the other.

What sort of clothes will they be wearing?

Photocopiables

Skinny people, see page 106

Moore and Giacometti

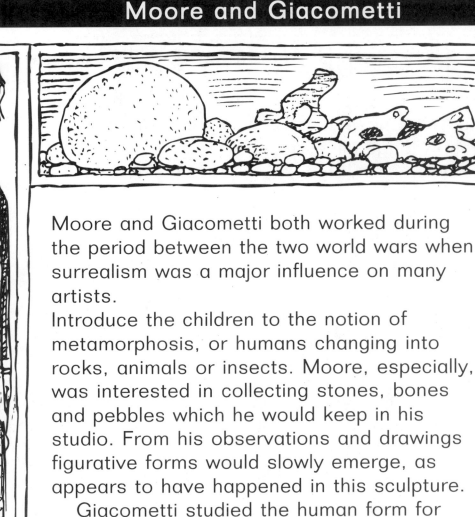

Moore and Giacometti both worked during
the period between the two world wars when
surrealism was a major influence on many
artists.

Introduce the children to the notion of
metamorphosis, or humans changing into
rocks, animals or insects. Moore, especially,
was interested in collecting stones, bones
and pebbles which he would keep in his
studio. From his observations and drawings
figurative forms would slowly emerge, as
appears to have happened in this sculpture.

Giacometti studied the human form for
many years, undertaking both searching
drawings as well as sculptures. In all of his
work there is an intensity of silence, figures
stare ahead, expressionless, having a
timeless quality shared only perhaps with
Egyptian sculpture.

Use the poster of both sculptures to
explore the importance of texture as an
element in three-dimensional work.

Skinny people, see page 106

Moore and Giacometti – key questions

1 Look carefully at the two sculptures. Where do you think would make an interesting place to put them?

2 Can you make a list of words which best describe the textures of the two sculptures? If you could run your hands over them how would the sculptures feel?

3 Both sculptures are of people, but what else do they remind you of? If these people were in a science fiction film, what do you think they might be turning into?

4 Do you think the sculptors worked from people modelling for them or do you think they were from the artists' imagination?

5 If these figures could come to life how do you think they might move? What sort of actions would they make? Can you imagine how they might walk?

6 Do you find these sculptures cheerful or sad? How do they make you feel?

7 How many ways can you think of in which these two sculptures are similar and in which ways are they different?

8 The sculptors have made it very difficult for us to see the faces of these three people. Can you draw a picture of their faces to show us more clearly how they might look in real life?

INFORMATION TECHNOLOGY WITHIN ART AT KEY STAGE 1

Art is very much a practical subject and although computers can enhance and extend children's experiences in this area, they should not replace the opportunity for practical hands-on exploration and experimentation with the full range of mark-making materials, tone, texture and colour. Indeed these early experiences will be essential if children are to make effective use of art and drawing software on computers at a later time. It is also important for children to have a real purpose in using art software if they are to explore the full benefits of computer graphics.

The work of other artists provides a rich source of ideas, examples and creativity and children can make use of information technology to find, store and use such works of art. CD-ROMs can contain many hundreds of pictures that can be displayed on screen or printed out. The Internet is now a rich source of both pictures and information about different artists. Both can be used to develop children's artistic skills.

Drawing and art packages

A vast array of art software is available for children of all ages. Some is very simple and suitable for young children. However as they progress or move on to more sophisticated drawing they can quickly become limited by a restricted range of options, for example having only 16 colours to chose from.

Throughout this book two distinct types of software have been identified: drawing or art software. Although they can often achieve similar results they have distinct differences which often makes them more suitable for particular activities. **Drawing packages** – These enable children to draw lines and shapes that can be manipulated, resized, moved, stretched and rotated. A range of colours can be selected and used to fill shapes. On more sophisticated packages the shapes can be combined to form a single 'object', so, for example, all the components of a flower can be drawn separately, combined and then kept as a flower. Text can be added and fonts, sizes and colours changed. In such packages it is easy to move shapes around the screen and position components of a picture wherever you wish. In order to help children line up the shapes and lines as they draw them it is usually possible to have a background grid. When the 'snap to grid' option is turned on, the ends of the drawn lines are automatically joined to the nearest point on the background grid. This makes it useful for lining up shapes in a pattern.

Art or painting packages – These use a different approach, where the drawing process is more akin to using a pencil or brush. Lines and shapes are drawn by colouring in the individual pixels of the screen. Very detailed work and effects can be produced to create pictures which, with skill, can mirror the results of paint on paper. Such packages usually have a range of tools such as brushes, sprays and rollers for adding and creating different effects. Text can be added, coloured and resized. Bear in mind that the saved pictures often take up large amounts of memory. Pictures taken from a CD-ROM or from the Internet will be in a format that will enable them to be viewed from within an art package.

The skills that children need to be taught using such software are similar to word processing, but related to pictures. The children will need to know how to:

• select appropriate tools for: line drawing (to draw thin and detailed lines); drawing straight and curved lines using freehand tools; brushes (to draw thicker lines); sprays (to spray colours or create a different line effect); rollers (to fill in areas of colour);

• change features of different tools to affect: the thickness of lines; the size and shape of brushes; the density of sprays;

• draw different lines and shapes including squares; rectangles; circles and ellipses;

• edit and erase shapes and lines to duplicate shapes or use a 'stamp' facility;

• use the undo facility to erase the last action;

• resize, rotate and move shapes and lines;

• fill shapes with colours;

• select colours from a simple or complex palette;

• add, resize and colour text;

• clear the screen or start again;

• save and retrieve their work from a disk;

• set up the printer and print out their work.

Using pictures from other sources

In this book the work of other artists is used to highlight particular techniques or approaches. High quality pictures are now available from many CD-ROMs and can be downloaded from the Internet.

Suitable pictures can be found on many CD-ROMS, some, such as *Art in the National Curriculum,* are compilations specially prepared for the National Curriculum, while others such as Microsoft's *Art Gallery* simply provide a large collection of pictures. The pictures can usually be saved from the CD-ROM onto the hard disk and then loaded into a suitable viewer or art package. They can then be printed out or viewed on screen. Although the final quality is not as good as a photograph or print these can be used to extend the range of available pictures. Children can also 'browse' the pictures to see a wider range from a particular artist.

In a similar way pictures can be downloaded from a whole host of Internet sites. Some sites are dedicated to a particular artist or period, whilst others provide pictures from a full range of artists. Teachers can use a search engine to locate such sites and save suitable pictures onto disk. A useful starting point could be sites found at:

http://www.oir.ucf.edu/wm/

http://www2.iinet.com/art/index.html

These sites have alphabetical lists of artists with a selection of thumbnail pictures. By selecting an appropriate thumbnail a full page version is shown, which can then be downloaded and saved onto a disk.

Access to a whole range of online galleries with different themes or ideas (including artists and sculptors) is at: http://netfind.aol.com/aol/Reviews/Arts/Fine_Arts/Galleries/Virtual_Galleries/index.netfind.html

Many other sites also include background information on artists and their works which can be useful for teachers' own knowledge and information.

Word Processing

Children could use a word processor throughout their art work to produce suitable labels for their work. This requires little keyboard time, but gives children an opportunity to select appropriate fonts, styles and sizes and present their label in a suitable style for the picture they have drawn. Older children could add information on particular artists or write larger descriptive labels about the techniques used to create their pictures.

Grids

The grids below relate the activities in this book to specific areas of IT and to relevant software resources. Activities are referenced by page number. The software listed in the second grid is a selection of programs generally available to primary schools, and is not intended as a recommended list. The software featured should be available from most good educational software retailers.

AREA OF IT	SOFTWARE	ACTIVITIES (page nos.)				
		CHAPTER 1	CHAPTER 2	CHAPTER 3	CHAPTER 4	CHAPTER 5
Communicating Info	Word Processor		38			
Communicating Info	Art	16, 18, 21, 29, 34	40, 42, 44, 47, 49, 52, 54	60, 62, 65, 67, 70, 75	78, 84, 85	101
Communicating Info	Drawing	29	40, 52, 54	60, 62, 67, 75		101
Communicating Info	Framework software			60		
Communicating Info	Authoring software	21				
Information handling	Internet	All	All	All	All	All
Information handling	CD-ROM	All	All	All	All	All

	BBC/MASTER	ROSCOS	NIMBUS/186	WINDOWS	MACINTOSH
Word processor	Stylus Folio Prompt/writer	Phases Pendown Desk Top Folio	All Write Write On	My Word Kid Works 2 Creative Writer	Kid Works 2 Easy Works Creative Writer
Framework		My World		My World	
Art package	Picture Builder	1st Paint Kid Pix Splash	Picture Builder	Colour Magic Kid Pix 2 Microsoft Paint	Kid Pix 2 Microsoft Paint Claris Works
Drawing package	Picture Builder	Draw Picture IT	Picture Builder	Claris Works Microsoft Draw	Claris Works Microsoft Draw
CD-ROM		Art in the National Curriculum		Art in the National Curriculum Art Gallery	Art Gallery

	ENGLISH	MATHS	SCIENCE	HISTORY	GEOGRAPHY	D&T	RE	MUSIC	PE
LINE	Describing observation of pictures. Expressing moods. Writing descriptions of pictures.	Areas, shapes, patterns, looking around the school.	Living processes. Looking at fruit, vegetables and plants and recording observations.		Looking at lines on a map. Explaining contours.	Designing by undertaking line drawing. For example drawings of bikes.	Exploring feelings. Moods – happy and sad. Family relationships. Madonna and child.	Music to reflect moods: happy, sad, composing and performing.	Exploring how to move like different animals. Shapes and balances. Exploring shape in gymnastics.
COLOUR	Developing precision in language. Using specific words to describe colours. Developing imaginative words.	Investigating pattern in nature.	Living processes. Observing changes in the colour of vegetables, fruit etc when decaying.	Understanding time – looking at the work of Van Gogh.	Exploring colour in geography, for example infra red pictures, symbols on maps.	Designing and making boxes, for example to package some flowers.	Working in small groups and pairs, sharing materials.	Interpreting ideas of sounds eg 'Stormy seas, sunny skies'. Listening and appreciating music.	
PATTERN	Writing stories for example to illustrate drawings, for example, 'Lost in the forest'.	Simple mathematical shape recognition. Exploring shape.	Living processes. Looking for pattern in animals, birds, insects and plants.	Exploring buildings. Looking at changing styles and features, 'Patterns in buildings'.	Patterns in maps. Patterns in hedgerows, fields and towns.	Designing fabrics and making simple clothing.	Exploring the beauty of nature.	Patterns in pitch and rhythm. Learning simple rhythms to clap and play.	Exploring patterns through movement and balance working with a partner.
TEXTURE	Making a list of various textures. Describing words linked to their texture.		Materials and their properties, exploring the textural properties of materials.	Rubbings of churches and churchyards. Looking at the effect of ageing. Exploring concept of age.	Looking at the 'texture' of clouds, observing weather.	Textiles/ weaving. Designing and making a wall hanging.	Looking at old age and caring for old people.	Listening to music and exploring texture of various sounds.	
FORM	Writing a short play linked to mask making or acting out an improvised play.	3D form, explanation eg cones, pyramids. Measuring and estimating. Mathematical shapes.	Physical processes. Observing and recording changes to salt dough, clay etc.		Exploring where clay comes from. Discussing various uses for clay.	Exploring structure of materials, for example how strong a paper structure can	Working together in pairs to produce an item.	Producing sounds on various instruments to use in a play to mask making.	Examining the human form. Making figure drawings.